W01113791

BENJAMIN HARRISON
PRESIDENTIAL SITE

BENJAMIN HARRISON

The 23rd President

HARRISON'S LIFE AND LEGACY
AS TOLD THROUGH HIS HISTORIC HOME

DK LONDON

Senior Editor Fleur Star
Project Art Editor Gregory McCarthy
U.S. Editor Lori Cates Hand
Production Editor Robert Dunn
Production Controller Stephanie Kull
Art Director Maxine Pedliham
Publishing Directors Georgina Dee, Liz Wheeler

Special Sales and Custom Publishing Managers
Michelle Baxter, Lindsay Kent

DK DELHI

Editor Ekta Chadha
Art Editor Arshti Narang
Senior Managing Editor Rohan Sinha
Managing Art Editor Sudakshina Basu
Assistant Picture Researcher Nunhoih Guite
Senior Picture Researcher Sumedha Chopra
Picture Research Manager Taiyaba Khatoon
DTP Designers Raman Panwar, Vikram Singh
DTP Coordinator Tarun Sharma
Hires Coordinator Neeraj Bhatia
Jacket Designer Tanya Mehrotra
Pre-production Manager Balwant Singh
Production Manager Pankaj Sharma
Creative Head Malavika Talukder

Writer Contributor Mark Collins Jenkins

BENJAMIN HARRISON PRESIDENTIAL SITE

President and CEO Charles A. Hyde
Vice President of Curatorship and Exhibition Jennifer Capps
Vice President of Advancement Bethany Gosewehr
Vice President of Education Roger Hardig
Special Events and Marketing Manager Lindsey Beckley
Project Intern Jason Housley

First American Edition, 2025
Published in the United States by DK Publishing,
a division of Penguin Random House LLC
1745 Broadway, 20th Floor, New York, NY 10019

Copyright © 2025 Dorling Kindersley Limited
25 26 27 28 29 10 9 8 7 6 5 4 3 2 1
001–348341–May/2025

All rights reserved.
Without limiting the rights under the copyright reserved above, no part of this
publication may be reproduced, stored in or introduced into a retrieval system,
or transmitted, in any form, or by any means (electronic, mechanical, photocopying,
recording, or otherwise), without the prior written permission of the copyright owner.

A catalog record for this book is available from the Library of Congress.
ISBN 978-0-5939-7062-1

DK books are available at special discounts when purchased in bulk
for sales promotions, premiums, fund-raising, or educational use.
For details, contact: DK Publishing Special Markets,
1745 Broadway, 20th Floor, New York, NY 10019
SpecialSales@dk.com

Printed and bound in China

www.dk.com

MIX
Paper | Supporting
responsible forestry
FSC™ C018179

This book was made with Forest
Stewardship Council™ certified
paper—one small step in DK's
commitment to a sustainable future.
Learn more at **www.dk.com/uk/
information/sustainability**

CONTENTS

HOW THIS BOOK WORKS

This biography of Benjamin Harrison tells the story of the 23rd president through his home—the Benjamin Harrison Presidential Site. The book takes you on a tour of the house and uses objects found in the rooms to talk about the events and people that were important in his life. The book starts with information about Harrison and his Indianapolis neighborhood then and now, before exploring the house and artifacts. It finishes with his legacy and the Site today.

THE LIFE AND TIMES OF BENJAMIN HARRISON

Known to history as the "Hoosier President," Benjamin Harrison was the only U.S. chief executive to hail from Indiana. His political career spanned the Gilded Age from the 1860s to the 1890s. This era was known for its economic growth, creating both challenges and opportunities for Harrison, whose policies changed the United States in important ways.

Harrison was born on August 20, 1833, in North Bend, Ohio, at his grandfather William Henry Harrison's spacious estate, but he grew up on a farm a few miles down the Ohio River. In his early years he was tutored at home and, when

AGE 21, FRATERNITY PORTRAIT

Birthplace

Harrison was born in his grandfather's imposing house on the Ohio River, near Cincinnati. It was a landmark for passing steamships. This engraving shows an artist's idyllic version of North Bend, Ohio.

not doing chores, spent time reading, hunting, or fishing. Benjamin was too young to join family members in Washington, D.C. in March 1841 for the inauguration of his grandfather, the ninth president, who would die only a month into his term. William Henry Harrison—soldier, statesman, and former governor of the Indiana Territory—came from a patrician Virginia family with a long tradition of military and civic leadership. Benjamin's own father, John Scott Harrison, served two terms in Congress.

Heritage mattered to Benjamin Harrison. His mother, Elizabeth Irwin, came from a prominent Pennsylvania family. They had immigrated from Scotland and, unlike the Episcopalian Harrisons, were staunchly Presbyterian. Young Ben chose the leadership of one parent and the Presbyterianism of the other. He fell in love with books in his

Political parentage

Benjamin's grandfather William Henry Harrison was a general, a diplomat, Governor of the Indiana Territory, a senator, and the ninth President of the United States. Save for the governorship, his grandson would follow in his footsteps.

grandfather's library and was schooled in log houses before studying law at Miami University near Oxford, Ohio, and with a law firm in Cincinnati. It was while still a student that he met Caroline "Carrie" Scott, daughter of Presbyterian minister and university professor Dr. John Scott. Harrison saw in Carrie a like-minded but much more artistically talented partner. She saw in him an honest ambition and the will to succeed. Where he could be reserved, she was sociable. They married after he graduated, and by 1854, the Harrisons were westward bound to the growing city of Indianapolis.

Harrison did not find it easy to build his law career. He worked long hours, sometimes to the point of exhaustion, and was so thorough in his

Family comes first

In this 1889 depiction of the First Family at home, Caroline and Benjamin Harrison are flanked by their children, Russell and Mary, known as Mamie. Portraits on the wall are thought to show William Henry Harrison on the left and either his father, Benjamin Harrison V, or possibly George Washington on the right.

TIMELINE

1833 Born on August 20 in North Bend, Ohio, the second of the ten children of John Scott and Elizabeth Harrison.

1841 His grandfather, William Henry Harrison, is inaugurated as the ninth President of the United States, but dies a month later.

1852 Graduates from Miami University, Ohio, aged 19. Member of Phi Delta Theta fraternity.

MIAMI UNIVERSITY'S HARRISON HALL, RENAMED IN 1931 FOR THE SCHOOL'S FAMOUS ALUMNUS

1853 Marries Caroline Lavinia Scott on October 20.

1854 His first child, Russell Benjamin Harrison, is born in Ohio on August 12.

1854 Passes the Ohio bar examination, but chooses to move to Indianapolis with his family.

1855 Enters a partnership with William Wallace to form the law office of Wallace and Harrison.

RUSSELL HARRISON

1856 Joins the new Republican Party, supporting its candidate, General John C. Fremont, for President.

1857 Elected the City Attorney for Indianapolis, his first foray into public office.

1858 His daughter Mary Scott "Mamie" Harrison is born on April 3 in Indianapolis.

MARY HARRISON

research that, in one poisoning case, he questioned the doctors with so much detail that he, not the murder, became the sensation in the courtroom. His law practice with William Wallace was eventually successful, but both Harrison's family life and legal career were soon clouded by the gathering storm that would escalate into the Civil War in 1861. Despite his Virginian ancestry, Benjamin was avowedly a Midwesterner, a Republican, and a Unionist. At the Indiana governor's urging, he organized the 70th Indiana Regiment, becoming a lieutenant first, then a captain, and finally a colonel. He helped lead the regiment throughout the ferocious combat of the 1864 Atlanta campaign. At age 31 he was given a brigade to command, though his commission as brigadier, signed by President Abraham Lincoln, took months to arrive.

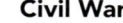

Civil War
"Come on, boys!" cries Harrison in this 1880s illustration of the Battle of Resaca (May 13–16, 1864). Benjamin Harrison led his 70th Indiana Regiment, and then the entire First Brigade, often in hand-to-hand fighting—but on foot, not on horseback as depicted here.

Post-war, back in Indianapolis, the General grew increasingly prominent in the legal and political circles of the city. Prosperity duly followed. When Harrison was in his early 40s, he and Caroline built the elegant Italianate brick mansion on North Delaware Street that would play a pivotal role through the rest of his life. Throughout these years, Harrison's eye was increasingly on politics. He undertook an unsuccessful run for governor, but his star was nevertheless rising. In 1880, the state legislature sent him to Washington to serve in the U.S. Senate.

Get the ball rolling
A Harrison supporter poses with a gigantic campaign ball that was rolled during the Presidential run. The phrase "get the ball rolling" may have originated with Benjamin's grandfather William Henry Harrison's similar Victory Balls in 1840.

From Senator to President
Pandemonium reigns at the Republican National Convention in Chicago when former Senator Benjamin Harrison, Indiana, and Levi P. Morton, New York, win the Presidential and Vice-Presidential nominations. Harrison won the nomination on the eighth ballot.

Case overload
This 1888 photograph of Harrison's office shows his desk teeming with books and legal documents, illustrating his busy and successful career as a lawyer.

Harrison's friends thought of him as genial and amiable, and to his family he was always loving and indulgent. However, strangers often found him cold; a "human iceberg" with the stern demeanor of a Presbyterian elder. The secret of Harrison's success was not due to affability, but rather his spellbinding oratory. This was never more evident than in the long summer of 1888 when he made his run for the U.S. presidency. Headquartered in his North Delaware Street home, Harrison conducted a "Front Porch" campaign. He stood on his stoop, speaking to crowds and stressing "Rejuvenated Republicanism" and the importance of high tariffs, spending budget surpluses, and adequate pensions for Civil War veterans. In a divided country, it was a message that appealed to enough Americans that, on November 6, when incumbent Grover Cleveland won the popular vote, Harrison triumphed in the Electoral College and won the presidency.

Harrison's was touted as the "Centennial Presidency" because it began 100 years after the first term of George Washington, the first

1860 Elected Reporter of Decisions of the Indiana Supreme Court; Wallace becomes the clerk of the Marion County Court.

INDIANA REPORTS

1860 Becomes partners with William Fishback in Fishback and Harrison.

1860 Works on behalf of Republican Abraham Lincoln during the Presidential campaign.

1862 Volunteers for service in the Civil War, forms the 70th Indiana regiment, and becomes its colonel.

70TH INDIANA REGIMENT AT HARRISON'S INAUGURATION

1864 During the Atlanta Campaign, leads his regiment in a successful charge in the Battle of Resaca.

1864 His brigade repulses the main Rebel attack at the Battle of Peachtree Creek during the Atlanta Campaign.

1864 His brigade engages in the Union assault that wins the Battle of Nashville.

1865 Brevetted a brigadier by Lincoln in January, and after hostility ceased is mustered out of service.

1868 The Harrisons buy land on North Delaware Street, an upscale Indianapolis neighborhood.

1875 Construction of the Harrisons' spacious new brick house on North Delaware Street is completed.

1876 Becomes the Republican nominee for Governor of Indiana, but loses in the general election.

1879 Appointed to the new Mississippi River Commission—a seven-member federal oversight body—by President Rutherford B. Hayes.

1881 Officially becomes a senator, having won a U.S. Senate race the previous autumn.

1888 On November 6, wins the election, defeating Grover Cleveland in the Electoral College, 233 to 168.

A WINNING CAMPAIGN BUTTON

1889–1893 Benjamin Harrison's term as the 23rd President of the United States.

U.S. President. A rainstorm marked inauguration day, nearly drowning out Harrison's Inaugural Address. In his speech, he charted with remarkable clarity the course his administration would follow. He promised a high tariff to protect American industries from foreign competition. He also upheld the moral necessity of providing pensions to Civil War veterans and their widows. Harrison advocated early statehood for the territories, the modernization of the Navy and Merchant Marine, continued noninterference in other nations' affairs, and adherence to the Monroe Doctrine of resisting European nations' interference in North and South American politics. Then Harrison relocated his family into the crowded family rooms of the White House and set to work.

The agenda Harrison set is the one he followed, with positive actions enlarging the U.S. Navy, bettering relations with Latin America, and building the foundations for forest conservation. He also signed into law the Tariff Act, which was so unpopular due to the resulting rise in the cost of goods that the Republicans lost the 1890 midterm Congressional elections. Even Harrison's 1891 cross-country train tour—the "Trip to Unify"—could not remedy this. To make matters worse, in early 1892, his reelection year, Caroline was diagnosed with tuberculosis and died in October. This led to a very subdued campaign on both sides, and Grover Cleveland returned to the White House while Harrison returned home to North Delaware Street.

Seafaring legacy
Sailors row President Harrison to the foot of New York's Wall Street in April 1889. Harrison's determination to expand the U.S. Navy's fleet led to the building of the first modern battleship, the USS *Indiana* (BB-1).

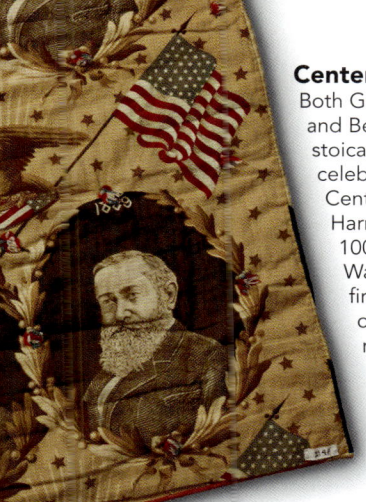

Centennial president

Both George Washington and Benjamin Harrison gaze stoically from this quilt celebrating the latter's Centennial Presidency. Harrison was inaugurated 100 years after George Washington became the first to take the Oath of Office. That led to national celebrations and lent an air of gravitas to the Harrison administration.

After his presidency, Harrison settled into his library and his comfortable law practice. However, in want of companionship, at the age of 67 he married his wife's niece, Mary Lord Dimmick—a young widow of 37 who had lived with them in Washington. The couple had one daughter, Elizabeth. This marriage strained his relationship with his other children. When Harrison died in 1901, he was surrounded by loved ones, but his adult children were unable to make it in time

Second family

After the death of Caroline Harrison, the bereaved ex-President fell in love with her niece, Mary Lord Dimmick (right), and married her in 1896. They had one child, Elizabeth Harrison (left).

1889 North Dakota, South Dakota, Montana, and Washington are admitted to the Union.

44 STATE U.S. FLAG

1890 Idaho and Wyoming are admitted to the Union, which now comprises 44 states.

1890 The Sherman Silver Purchase Act fails to satisfy farmers' and miners' hopes to mint silver coins.

1890 Signs the Tariff Act, increasing average duties on imports from 38% to 49.5%.

1891 Gives nearly 150 speeches on the "Trip to Unify," a 10,000-mile, 21-state train tour of the nation.

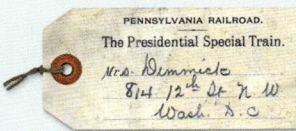

TRAIN LUGGAGE LABEL

1891 Signs the Forest Reserve Act of 1891, giving the President authority to unilaterally reserve forestlands in the public domain.

1892 On October 25, First Lady Caroline Scott Harrison, 60, dies of tuberculosis.

1892 Campaigns for reelection, but loses to Grover Cleveland on November 8.

1896 Marries Mary Lord Dimmick, 37, the niece of his first wife, Caroline Harrison.

1897 His daughter, Elizabeth Harrison, is born on February 21.

1897 *This Country of Ours*, Harrison's collected essays from the *Ladies' Home Journal* on how government works and the duties of citizenship, is published.

FIRSTHAND CIVICS

1901 Dies on March 13 and is buried in Indianapolis' Crown Hill Cemetery.

TOMBSTONE OF BENJAMIN HARRISON

1948 Mary Dimmick Harrison, 89, dies in New York City and is buried alongside Benjamin in Crown Hill Cemetery.

HARRISON'S INDIANAPOLIS

In the early 19th century, Indianapolis was largely a tract of forest, its streets and squares plotted and planned only on paper. By the time Benjamin Harrison moved with his family in April 1854, it had become a bustling town of 8,000 people, with schools, churches, newspapers, and a state capitol (Statehouse) resembling the Parthenon in Athens, Greece. By 1875, when work on the Harrisons' house was complete, Indianapolis had transformed into a metropolis with a population of 75,000 and a regional railroad hub second only to Chicago, Illinois. In 1888, when Harrison was running for the nation's highest office, work had begun on the city's iconic Soldiers and Sailors Monument, dedicated to Indiana citizens who had fought in various wars of the past, and a grand Union Station had just opened. The original Statehouse building was replaced in 1888 with the one that stands today. This is where Harrison's body would lie in state after his death in 1901.

This engraving shows the sumptuous interior of Union Station as it appeared around 1889.

Union Station, Indianapolis

In 1853, Indianapolis erected the first "union" station in the United States as a railroad hub for the Midwest, serving multiple railroad lines. In 1888, the original building was replaced by a grand terminal. Around 200 trains passed through daily, serving 500,000 passengers a month—the largest interurban train station in the world.

Washington Street, Indianapolis at Dusk

In this evening scene painted between 1892 and 1895, German artist Theodor Groll depicts the new Statehouse as it looms over the carriages, streetcars, and market stalls of Washington Street, the heart of downtown Indianapolis.

Modern Indianapolis

The once towering Statehouse building is dwarfed by skyscrapers in downtown Indianapolis today. As a center of politics, economy, and culture, Indianapolis has not ceased growing. The city's population tops 880,000; more than 2 million live in the greater metropolitan area.

Vance Block

This flatiron, or triangular-shaped, office building was designed by William H. Brown in 1875. Clad in limestone, it featured an 80-foot tower and an open atrium. The building also boasted Indianapolis's first elevator.

Moving toward modernity

Transportation is a key component of urban growth. Streetcars in Indianapolis were powered by horses or mules until the late 19th century. By the 1890s, streetcars were running on electricity.

City Market and Tomlinson Hall

This vintage postcard depicts the Indianapolis marketplace and Tomlinson Hall, a public meeting space. Harrison's second wife, Mary, caused quite a sensation by personally visiting the market in order to buy groceries for the family.

OLD NORTHSIDE

Northeast of downtown Indianapolis is the historic district of the Old Northside. Benjamin Harrison purchased a double lot of land on the west side of North Delaware Street in 1868, starting construction of the house in 1874. In 1875, when the Harrisons moved in, it was one of the most affluent areas of the city and home to important community figures from the worlds of industry and commerce, politics, and literature, as well as churches and schools. It is noteworthy, though perhaps unsurprising, that many of Harrison's neighbors had a connection to him, often through his law work.

N. Delaware Street

This 1898 fire insurance map shows brick houses in pink and frame houses in yellow. Several of them no longer exist today. The descriptions of the houses use current street numbers.

❶ 1441, Milligan House

Harry J. Milligan studied law in the Harrison, Hines, and Miller law office in the 1870s. He married Caroline Fishback, daughter of William, who had lived at number 1101. They commissioned this house in 1895.

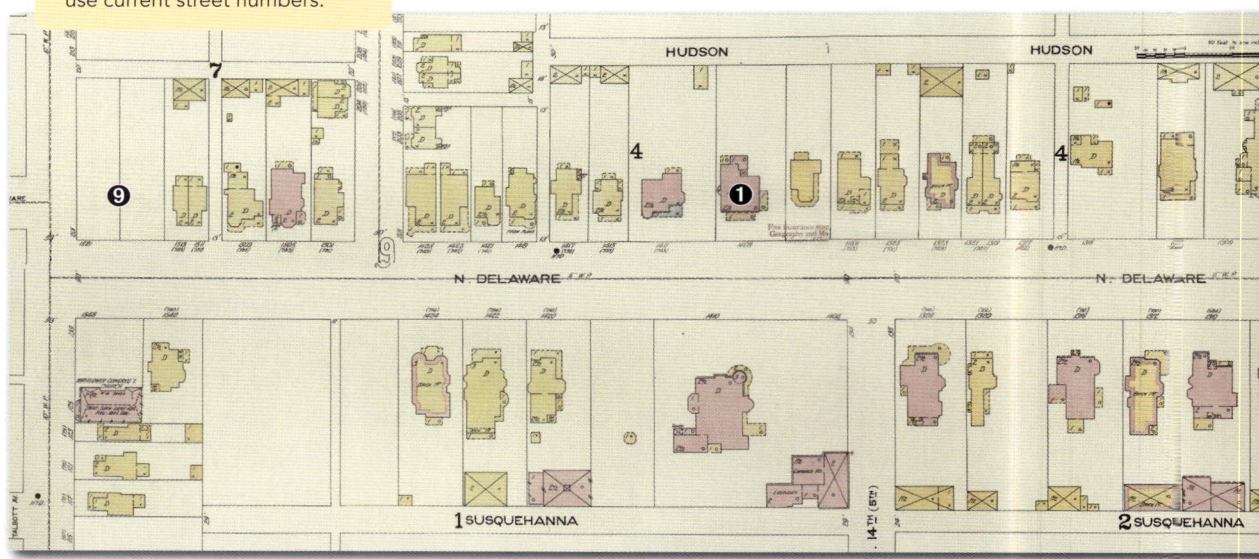

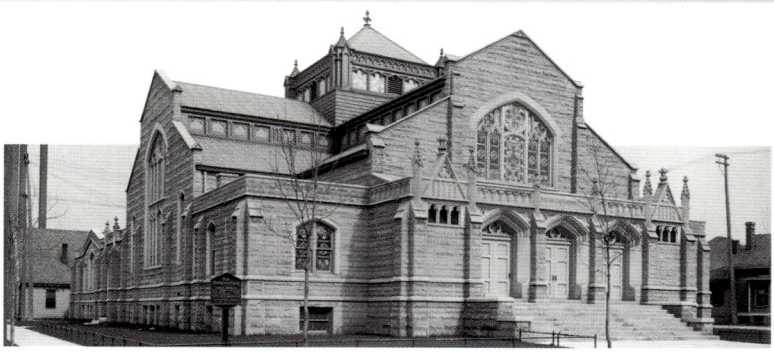

❾ 1525 Former First Presbyterian Church

The Harrisons were active members of the Presbyterian Church. This building, its fourth home, was constructed in 1903 in Gothic style. One of its windows—designed by Tiffany—was commissioned by Benjamin's widow, Mary.

❽ 1320, Duzan/Root/Wilson House

Where the Harrison Apartments stand today was this grand tower house, home to Dr. George Duzan, then Deloss Root, president of the Indianapolis Stove Co., then Medford B. Wilson, president of the Capital National Bank.

❷ 1229, Carey/McKee House

Stove-maker Jason Carey built this large Italianate cottage in 1873. Brothers General William and Edward McKee occupied the house from 1873. Another brother, Robert, married Harrison's daughter Mary.

❸ 1217, Spann/Miller House

Built by real estate and insurance agents Thomas and John Spann in 1874, William Henry Harrison Miller bought this house in 1879. Miller was Harrison's law partner and later Attorney General in his cabinet.

❹ 1101, Fishback House

William Pinckney Fishback was at Miami University in Ohio with Harrison, and became his partner in a law firm in 1861. At the time he lived here in the 1880s he worked for the federal courts in Indiana.

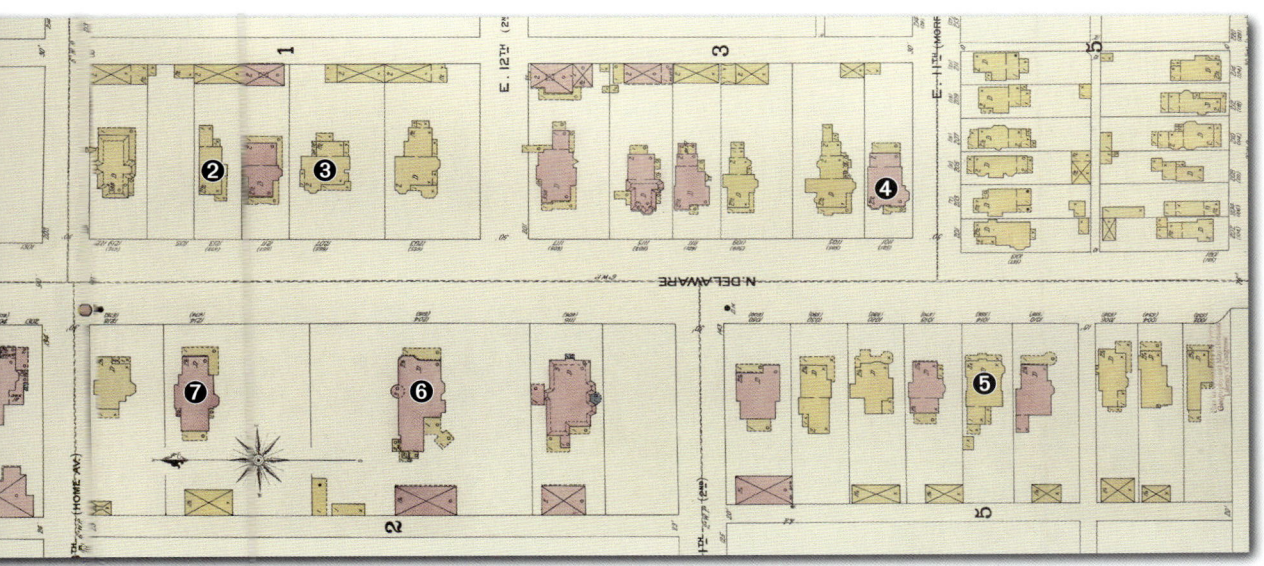

❼ 1230, Harrison House

When Harrison built the house, it was number 674, but numbering changed in 1893 (becoming 1214) and again in 1911. The Italianate style was designed by architect Herman T. Brandt, along with Caroline's input.

❻ 1204, Emery/Ayres House

The Harrisons' neighbors in this Queen Anne style brick house were George Emery, manufacturer of black walnut veneers, and Lyman S. Ayres. His store, L. S. Ayres & Co., became one of the city's leading department stores.

❺ 1028, Pierson/Griffiths House

Today known as Kemper House, this wooden home was built by dentist Charles Pierson. It was later lived in by diplomat John Griffiths, who nominated Harrison for senator from Indiana in 1881.

❶ Front parlor
See pages 24–25

❷ Back parlor
See pages 28–29

❸ Library
See pages 34–35

❹ Dining room
See pages 40–41

❺ Kitchen
See page 44

The back rooms were reserved for servants in Harrison's time.

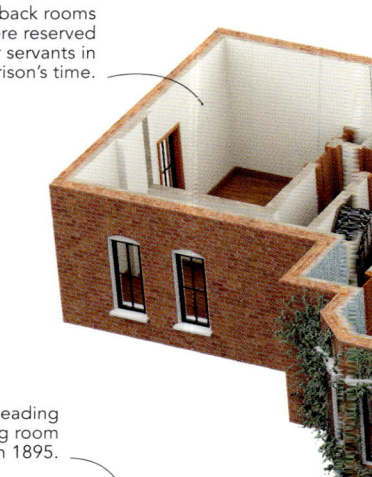

THE 1895 HOUSE

"Gen. Ben. Harrison proposes erecting a $15,000 dwelling on North Delaware street," read an item in one of the Indianapolis newspapers in 1873. The 16-room house was completed by 1875, but repairs were needed on Harrison's return from the White House in 1893; as he wrote to a friend, "My house needed the labor of almost every known trade." By 1895, front and rear porches and a two-story addition of a pantry and a bathroom were in place. Harrison wrote to his daughter, "I am dreadfully tired of all this bother ... & have resolved to stop when those things are done."

The butler's pantry leading into the dining room was expanded in 1895.

The wraparound front porch was added in 1894.

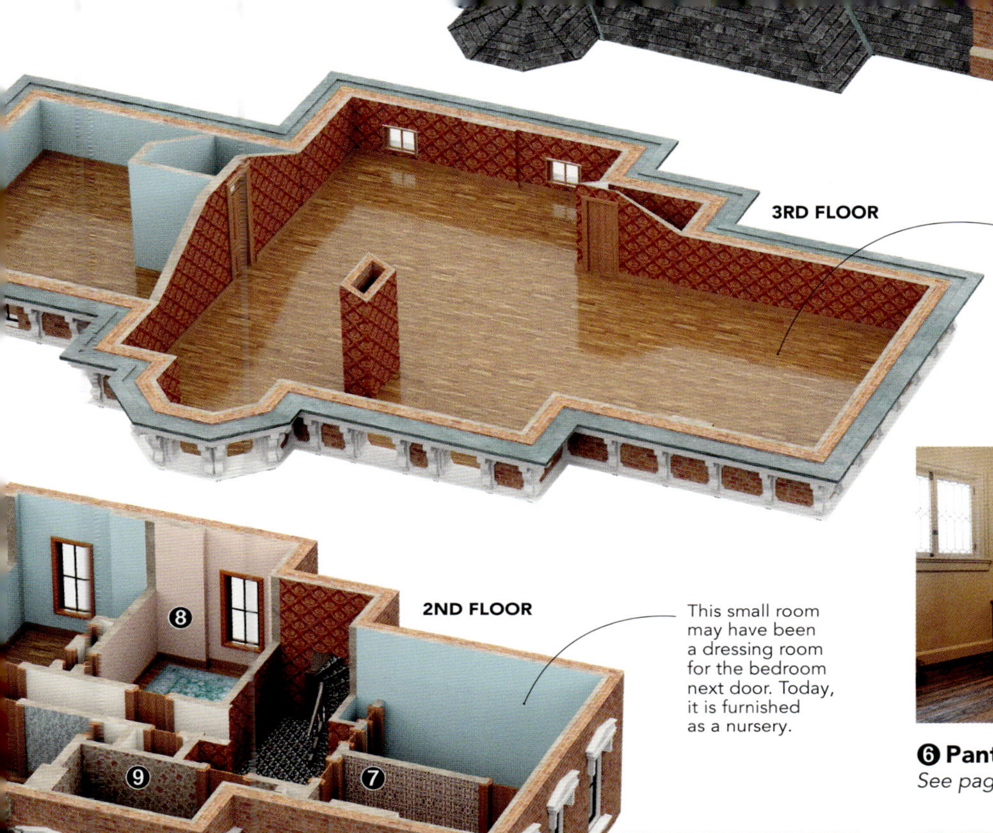

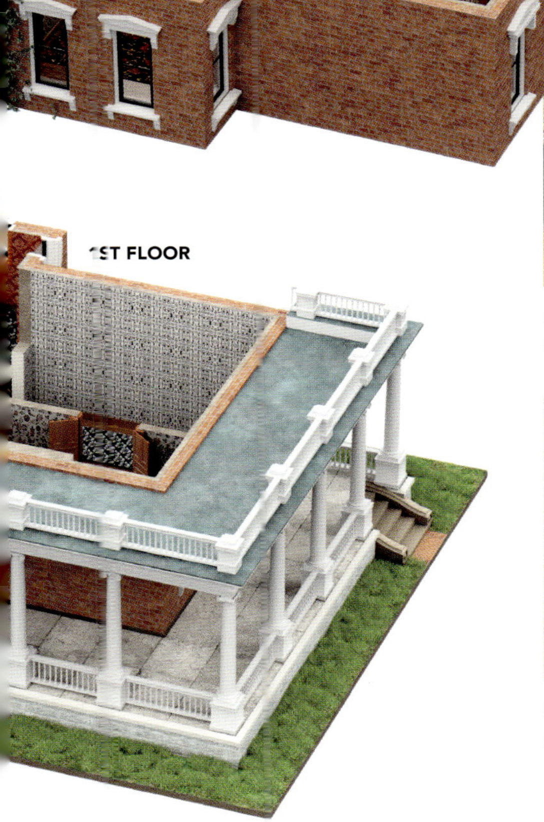

3RD FLOOR

The top floor was originally a ballroom. It is now used as an exhibit space and a research library for the Benjamin Harrison Presidential Site.

2ND FLOOR

This small room may have been a dressing room for the bedroom next door. Today, it is furnished as a nursery.

1ST FLOOR

❻ Pantry
See page 45

❼ Mary's bedroom
See pages 48–49

❽ Elizabeth's bedroom
See page 50

❾ Sitting room
See page 51

❿ The Harrisons' bedroom
See pages 54–55

THE GARDEN

When Benjamin and Caroline Harrison purchased the double lot of land on North Delaware Street, it must have been in their minds to set aside a generous amount of outdoor space. The largest lawn was to the south of the house. There were also trees, some shrubs, and flowers. The Harrisons also grew strawberries and grapes every year. The lot was surrounded by wooden fences until 1888 when people started taking pickets from the east fence (along N. Delaware Street) as souvenirs. Enough of the pickets were stolen that the entire fence was later removed.

The barn's loft, above the carriage hall and horse stalls, is thought to be where the groomsman and driver lived.

❶ **Carriage house**
This large red barn was where the Harrisons kept their horse and buggy. It was extended in 1893 and also equipped with a natural gas supply, a sink, and a water closet.

The large wooden arbor was used for growing grapes.

❷ **Arched arbor**
This photograph from 1900 shows Elizabeth Harrison, with her mother Mary, sitting under the wire arch of the honeysuckle arbor that was on the south lawn.

❹ **Garden statue**
This limestone statue, carved by Ferdinand Cross, was originally designed for the 1893 Columbian Exposition (also known as the Chicago World's Fair). It was made to hold plants, and today it forms the centerpiece of the Caroline Scott Harrison herb garden.

❸ **Sand pile**
Family photographs reveal that the sandbox was an important feature of the garden in Elizabeth Harrison's childhood. Here, she is the seated child seen playing with friends.

FERDINAND CROSS WITH THE STONE PLANTER

The 1895 garden

This illustration shows the area of the gardens from the time Benjamin Harrison lived at the house. The Site today is more than three times the size, covering land where houses once stood.

Elizabeth's roses

Behind the north side of the house (not visible in this illustration) is the Elizabeth Harrison Rose Garden, dedicated to Benjamin Harrison's mother. Designed by Frits Loonsten, it was built in 1973–1974.

The dotted lines show the area of the original garden at the time the Harrisons lived in the house.

The modern gardens

Today's garden areas were established by volunteers. There are some original plants, such as the peonies, strawberries, and mock orange in the Herb Garden ❺. The grapes in the Victorian Vintage Garden ❻ may date back to the Harrisons' time. There are hollyhocks from the 1800s in the Freedom Garden ❼, and an oak ❽ more than 100 years old.

ARCHITECTURE AND DESIGN

North Delaware Street in the 1870s was becoming a popular neighborhood and, after conferring with architect Herman T. Brandt, Harrison settled on a fashionable style for his new residence. The elegant and refined Italianate style, inspired by the architecture of Renaissance Italy, had replaced Greek Revival about the time of the Civil War and would remain popular until unseated by the Queen Anne style around 1890.

The three-story, 16-room house took nearly a year to complete. The total cost to build and furnish the home, including the later additions and improvements, was $29,000 (around $830,000

today). Indiana limestone two feet thick lined the basement, French-plate windows provided sunlight, and a few conveniences that were uncommon during this period were added: running water, a coal-fed furnace, 23 working gaslight fixtures, and 12-foot-high ceilings. When finished, it was indeed large—more than 12,600 square feet—handsome, yet "unpretentious," as many contemporaries described it. Windows were tall and narrow, and the hipped roof, with slate tiles, was wider than it was tall. The bricks were offset by stone trimmings and white cornices accentuated the deep eaves marking the roofline. The ornate features continued inside.

The bracketed cornice, projecting outward beneath the eaves, is a ubiquitous feature of the Italianate style in America. This cornice is made of sheet metal and painted gray.

DETAIL OF CORNICE

The front doorknob is surrounded by an elaborately designed, Eastlake-styled plate.

BRASS DOORKNOB

Viewing the facade

Looking at the house from Delaware Street, visitors see the harmonious balance between two architectural styles. The corbels (supporting brackets) and cornices above the door and along the roofline are Italianate style. Projecting toward the street is the front porch in Colonial Revival style with its noble Ionic columns. As a personal touch, the initials "B.H." are etched into the front door glass.

The 1893 house

This photograph of the Harrisons' house appeared in Ernest Percy Bicknell's book *Indianapolis Illustrated* in 1893. This is the year that Harrison returned to Indiana from the White House.

ROSETTES

BACK PARLOR CEILING MEDALLION

These zinc rosettes come from the frieze at the top of the outside wall.

Plaster brackets frame the archway in the staircase hall.

PLASTER BRACKET

All in the details

No detail was overlooked in the construction of the home, inside or out. The gas ceiling lights were suspended from decorative plasterwork, often molded with flower motifs. These were functional as well; the raised middle sloped toward the outer rim, helping the gas to disperse.

Parquet flooring

The floors in the two parlors and the library have parquet flooring with an inlay fashioned from birds-eye maple and mahogany. By the 1870s such elaborate flooring was a popular alternative to expensive fitted carpets.

21

Back parlor piano
Piano music was the primary source of entertainment during family gatherings. This mid-19th century square grand piano with octagonal legs and matching stool is similar to the one enjoyed by the Harrisons.

Visitors welcomed inside could gaze at walls and ceilings smoothed with plaster and accentuated by cornices, ceiling medallions, and other decorative features. Every room was wallpapered with bright colors and floral motifs, for this was an era when Americans were showing interest in this rising trend. The Harrisons' home sported wallpaper even on the ceilings, and some rooms had as many as four different wallpaper designs. No doubt the patterns reflected Caroline Harrison's taste and artistic eye.

The Indianapolis house served as Harrison's headquarters during his 1888 presidency campaign. That year he had a telegraph wire strung to the house, and the following year he had a telephone installed, just over a decade after its invention in 1876. Evenings in the Harrison home in the '70s and '80s were illuminated by gaslight supplemented by kerosene lamps and candles. After returning from the White House, which was wired for electricity during his tenure, Harrison added electricity to his Indianapolis home as well. Not all of the features were quite so high-tech: the Harrisons had an elaborate burglar alarm, which was a set of strings and bells attached to the doors.

After Harrison returned from the White House, he added a wraparound porch to the front of the house. It was designed by architect Louis H. Gibson in the Colonial Revival style—inspired by the colonial houses of the past—with Ionic columns supporting a classical structure with dentil (toothlike) moldings and balustrades on both the ground floor and the second story.

Embracing new technology

In 1889, the Harrisons installed a telephone making them one of the first residents in Indianapolis to own the instrument. They were listed in the city's telephone directory with the number 243.

Freestanding cookstove

This antique wood-burning stove stands in the kitchen today. It is similar to the Harrisons' freestanding cookstove that ran on coal until it was converted to gas in the 1890s.

The stovepipe would be vented outside through a chimney.

Ranges, or cooktops, relieved cooks from stooping over fireplaces while preparing meals on the hearth.

Snippet from the past

This scrap of original wallpaper was discovered behind the library bookcase during restoration in 1985. Experts studied the flowers-and-willow-leaves pattern and were able to recreate the design, which is typical of the type popular in America around 1870–1890.

Hand-crafted replica wallpaper covers the library walls today.

INSIDE THE LIBRARY

Newel lights

The gas lamp on the newel post at the foot of the main staircase resembles fixtures seen in catalogs from the 1870s. The lamp was later converted to electricity, likely in the mid 1890s.

FRONT PARLOR

In most fine 19th century houses, especially those of prominent public figures, the front parlor served as a formal reception area. When visitors cross the threshold into the Harrison household, they step into a spacious hall and turn left to enter perhaps the most striking room in the house. This was where the Harrisons would greet their visitors and guests.

The front parlor is not exactly the same as it was during the tumultuous days of the "Front Porch" campaign, having been redecorated in 1896 for Harrison's new bride, Mary Dimmick Harrison. Yet, even now, it remains equally elegant. The gilded frames and the magnificent rosewood piano still attract visitors today just as surely as they impressed friends of the Harrisons in the late 1890s.

The small, marble-topped table in the center of the room remains a mute witness to the excitement of that long-ago presidential campaign. Moreover, the pocket doors leading into the family parlor are the same ones Harrison stood beside when he formally accepted the Republican nomination for the nation's highest office on a memorable June afternoon in 1888.

The sprinkler incorporates bird motifs with a peacock feather pattern at its base, and a neck resembling that of a goose.

Perfume sprinkler
This wedding gift was presented to Harrison and his second wife, Mary, in 1896. The iridescent glass was developed by Louis Comfort Tiffany, the founder of Tiffany Studios, a glassmaking company.

Portrait of Benjamin Harrison, 1901
Noted Indiana painter T.C. Steele caught the devout, sober-suited, Bible-reading character of Benjamin Harrison in this painting, commissioned after he returned from the White House.

A formal welcome

The front parlor conveys an atmosphere of importance with many original features and artifacts, including the carved fireplace, chandelier, and rug.

Caroline Scott Harrison

This c. 1885 oil portrait of Harrison's first wife was painted by Lilly Martin Spencer, a popular 19th-century artist. Many engravings and prints would be made from this image of the soon-to-be First Lady.

Inaugural gift

This vase, gifted at Harrison's inauguration, characterizes the "American Art Pottery" movement that flourished in the late 19th century. It was sculpted by Albert Robert Valentien, the chief ceramics decorator at Rookwood Pottery, the first female-owned substantial manufacturing enterprise in the United States.

Dispensing aroma

A matching pair of porcelain jars, filled with dried flower petals and called "potpourri jars," grace the mantel of the fireplace. They were made in Budapest, then in the Austro-Hungarian Empire, and given to the Harrisons by a Hungarian friend.

Gold lions cap the jars, their mouths open so that the scent of flower petals can escape.

Red, blue, and yellow flowers are intertwined with green leaves and twisting vines.

FRONT PORCH CAMPAIGN

Throughout the 19th century, candidates for high political office often chose the "Front Porch" style of campaigning made popular by James A. Garfield. Benjamin Harrison revived this style during his presidential campaign. Harrison came to know that the Republicans had nominated him for president at their June 1888 National Convention. He was escorted home by throngs of supporters, and by the time he officially accepted the nomination while standing between his two parlors, thousands of people were in his yard. He stepped outside and gave a rousing speech. And so began his famous "Front Porch" campaign, where he delivered speeches from the front step of his house (an actual porch was added only in 1895). Dignitaries, delegations, journalists, and advisors descended daily. Harrison—a superb orator—would stand on his stoop to offer superlative impromptu remarks. In November, he won the election carrying the Electoral College 233 to 168.

ONE GOOD TERM DESERVES ANOTHER

HARRISON

THE TIPPECANOE RATTLER

& REID

The mention of Tippecanoe reminded voters that Harrison's grandfather had also been president. William Henry Harrison was known as Old Tippecanoe since winning the Battle of Tippecanoe in 1811.

The rattler's reverse side featured Whitelaw Reid, the Republican vice-presidential candidate.

Campaign memorabilia
Before the advent of mass media, one way to spread awareness was to have campaign souvenirs. The Tippecanoe Rattler was made for Harrison's 1892 reelection campaign. Despite the slogan "One Good Term Deserves Another," Harrison lost this election.

Man of the hour

Benjamin Harrison, engulfed by an excited throng of well-wishers and curiosity seekers, can hardly be seen in this photo. He is the bearded, short-statured man in the dark suit, standing on the front stoop.

Axing the opposition

Emblazoned with an assertive "Slayer of Free Trade," this homemade axe from New York State is a reference to Harrison's protectionist policies, as opposed to the Democrats' free-trade ones.

Political statement

Lapel pins have always been a popular means of displaying one's patriotism and were an essential part of Harrison's 1888 election campaign to rally support for himself and his running mate, Levi P. Morton.

A wreath of laurels was an elegant addition to campaign ephemera.

Family legacy

This campaign ribbon features William Henry Harrison's log cabin theme, reinforcing the connection between Benjamin and his grandfather. William had also used log cabin motifs in his own campaign posters.

BACK PARLOR

A pair of sliding "pocket" doors dividing the formal front parlor from the back one marked a transition between two worlds.

As guests stepped across the threshold from one stately parlor into a second, they entered the family space, often closed off from the public eye. The change was not immediately apparent because the furnishings were similar in style and arrangement, and there were also times when the pocket doors were left open to create a larger space for special events. It was in this doorway that Harrison stood and accepted his nomination for the presidency.

Nevertheless, the family room was a place where the Harrison family could relax, read, play games, discuss the news, gossip, and simply enjoy each other's company. It must have been a bustling place throughout the years when Harrison's children and grandchildren shared the home, especially on long winter evenings when snow blanketed the fields outside.

Interspersed among those years, however, were the six Harrison served in the U.S. Senate and the four years of

Trendy furniture

This Eastlake table appears in photographs of the house from as early as 1888. The style, which originated in England, had crossed the Atlantic by then. Eastlake style emphasized clean, sharp lines with graceful proportions, and much of the Harrisons' furniture is Eastlake in inspiration.

Ushering in electricity

After the White House was wired for electricity during Harrison's tenure, he had his Delaware Street house wired too.

The electrified chandelier fixture is original, while the type of glass shade changed over the years.

Space to socialize

Similar to the front parlor, the back parlor also features a fireplace but with dragon motifs in its mantel. The overhead electrolier (chandelier powered by electricity) illuminates the room.

This Reginaphone disk plays Sousa's "El Capitan" March. The word "Beginning" was stamped on it so listeners knew where to line up the comb to start playing the disk.

his presidency, when winters were spent in Washington because that is when the Congress convened.

In later years, the room entertained fewer family members. First Lady Caroline died in 1892—while Harrison still held office—and the others eventually moved out, leaving only Harrison, his second wife Mary, and their newborn daughter Elizabeth in the 10,000-square-foot residence.

Perforations in the revolving metal disk plucked teeth in the machine's comb, producing musical notes.

Creating music

Like other families of means, the Harrisons owned a piano for entertainment. Some families had a Reginaphone—a parlor-sized music box that worked in a similar way to a player piano, creating notes using a metal disk. Later, it could also be used to play phonograph records.

THE PRESIDENCY

Benjamin Harrison was inaugurated as the 23rd President of the United States on March 4, 1889. Though he only served one term, it was an ambitious four years.

Economics dominated Harrison's agenda. He was a high-tariff supporter, believing that protection of American industry against cheap foreign imports was the road to national prosperity.

In 1890, he signed into law the McKinley Tariff Act, raising the tax on imported goods while also adding reciprocity agreements (allowing nations to negotiate lower import rates in return for lower American export rates). At the same time, Congress passed the Sherman Silver Purchase Act, which obligated the government to purchase 4.5 million ounces of silver every month. This threatened the gold standard backing of the U.S. dollar, which roiled American politics. Harrison tried steering a middle course but failed to find acceptable solutions.

Among his other policies, Harrison pressed for greater civil rights for Black Americans in the South, but his efforts were met by resistance from Congress. His chief accomplishments were civil service reforms that based government employment on merit, higher pensions for Civil War veterans, establishing the U.S.

"My hand was placed here," Harrison notes in the margin by Psalm 121 of the Bible used for the administration of the Inaugural Oath.

National Forest system, and expanding the U.S. Navy into a world-class fleet.

Harrison's Administration convened the First International Conference of American States in 1889–1890 to improve cultural and diplomatic ties across the Western Hemisphere. It also established better relations with Latin America, although in October 1891, the country was at the brink of war with Chile when American sailors on shore leave in Valparaiso, Chile, were killed by an anti-U.S. mob. Harrison demanded Chile take responsibility and pay $75,000 in reparations; tensions abated when Chile agreed to the demands.

The 1893 cabinet (L–R): Stephen Elkins (War), John Noble (Interior), John Foster (State), John Wanamaker (Postmaster General), President Harrison, Benjamin Tracy (Navy), Charles Foster (Treasury), Jeremiah Rusk (Agriculture), William Miller (Attorney General).

The President's men

Harrison's cabinet, with Levi Morton (not pictured) as Vice President, changed little over time. In 1891, William Windom (Treasury) died and Redfield Proctor (War) moved to the Senate. In 1892, James Blaine (State) resigned to run against Harrison as the Republican presidential candidate. He lost.

Addressing the nation

Benjamin Harrison (at center, white-bearded, with top hat) delivered his short Inaugural Address in the rain as former president Grover Cleveland held an umbrella over him.

Menu of the banquet for the delegates, held in Chicago on October 22, 1889.

First International Conference

Delegates toured the States ahead of months of discussions in Washington D.C. The most abiding achievement of the Conference was the establishment of the Pan-American Union (today the Organization of American States.)

This ticket to Harrison's inauguration admits the holder to the "Senate floor and Platform."

The statue is made from more than 25,000 melted-down silver dimes donated by the public, many of them children.

In Memoriam

Charles W. Riggin, Boatswain's Mate on the USS *Baltimore*, was one of the sailors killed in Valparaiso. Three statues of him bearing the plaque "In Memoriam" were made by sculptor Alexander Doyle and presented to Harrison and his Secretaries of State and Navy.

TRIP TO UNIFY

One of the most politically memorable trips of President Harrison was the five-week tour he made from April 14 to May 15, 1891, journeying through the South to the West Coast and back to Washington. He traveled in a special train consisting of five opulent Pullman cars, with "The Presidential Special" styled in gold on the front one. It traversed through more than 20 states, making frequent stops before expectant crowds. Accompanied by the First Lady as well as Cabinet officials, the President would often speak from a covered platform on the observation car at the end. He gave 142 speeches throughout the trip.

Across the South and Southwest and up through California, Harrison was received with great enthusiasm. Coal-and-water stops provided speaking opportunities and, sometimes, he delivered speeches in pouring rain. Once, he spoke from a stand built on a redwood-tree stump. On the return trip, the company visited Abraham Lincoln's grave in Springfield, Illinois. The reception Harrison received during this trip fortified his belief in the unity of the nation.

Throngs of visitors listen to the President's speech in San Diego, California.

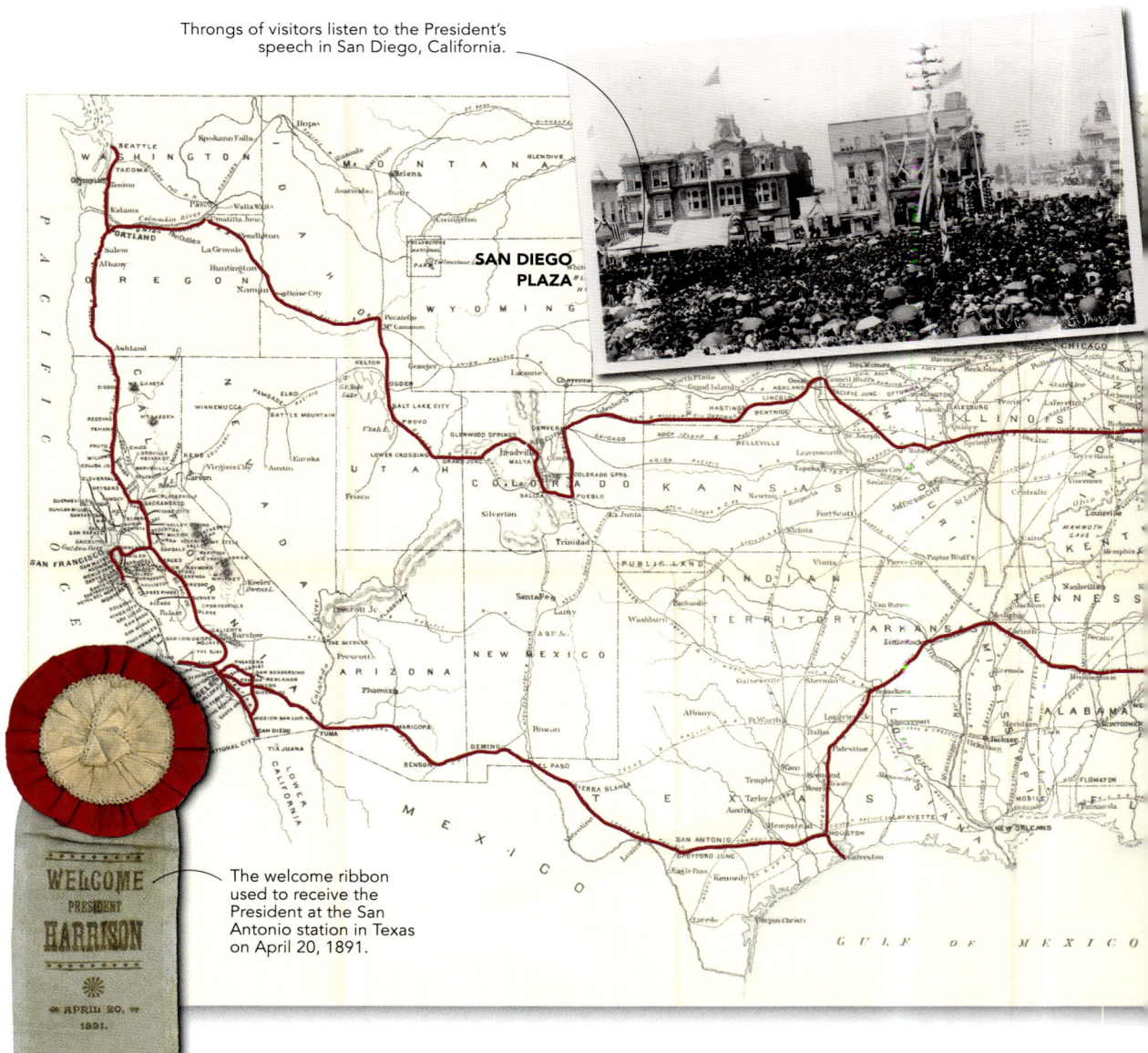

The welcome ribbon used to receive the President at the San Antonio station in Texas on April 20, 1891.

WELCOME PRESIDENT HARRISON

APRIL 20, 1891.

USS MONTEREY AXE

The honorary axe presented to "Mrs. B. Harrison," for cutting the ribbons during the launch ceremony.

There were two launch buttons on the table: one for the ship, and the other for the champagne!

Route map

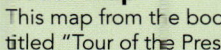

This map from the booklet titled "Tour of the President to the Pacific Coast" charts Harrison's unification tour of the nation. The thin red line follows the route of the trip that began from Washington.

Harrison's itinerary for April 14, 1891 shows how busy his schedule was.

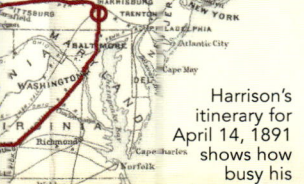

TOUR OF THE PRESIDENT TO THE PACIFIC COAST,
APRIL 14th to MAY 15th,
1891

TRIP ITINERARY

Launching the USS *Monterey*

On April 28, 1891, First Lady Caroline Harrison launched the USS *Monterey* in San Francisco, California. This heavily armed ship, assigned for coastal and harbor defense, was a part of Harrison's larger efforts to strengthen the U.S. Navy. Excitingly, it was launched using electric buttons.

Political observations

This woodcut appeared in black and white on the *Harper's Weekly* cover during the trip, when the train was still in California. Jeremiah Rusk (standing center), the Secretary of Agriculture, is conferring with President Harrison (seated right) in the observation car.

A reciprocal gift

Harrison also made a train trip for his inauguration. While in Richmond, Indiana, a young girl named Elizabeth Lida Jones gifted Harrison a silver penknife. Touched by this gesture, he sent her this porcelain doll the following Christmas.

LIBRARY

The library was Benjamin Harrison's favorite room. His book collection was his pride and joy, and Harrison did his most creative and incisive work when he was with his books. Featuring more than 3,000 titles, the heart of that collection still resides in the magnificent hand-carved walnut bookcase that dominates the library. It was made for him by a German cabinetmaker.

Mementoes and pictures abound in this room, including a portrait of Harrison's grandfather, William Henry Harrison, in whose own library young Benjamin first learned to love reading. Many of the items recall Harrison's later years in the White House, for it was in this room that much of his 1888 campaign for the presidency was planned.

His private secretary recorded a poignant moment spent here. On the very morning the family was to board the train, taking them all to the Inauguration in Washington, Harrison was found alone in the library with tears in his eyes. He eventually composed himself and said farewell to his neighbors and fellow citizens while proclaiming love for his adopted state, Indiana.

The "General Benjamin Harrison" gold nameplate is inset with diamonds.

Horn chair
This unique seat was an inaugural gift from Dennis O'Connor, a wealthy Texas rancher. Made of cattle horns screwed together, it features a jaguar-pelt seat, and plaques celebrating the Battles of Tippecanoe and the Alamo.

A place to ponder
The library housed some of Harrison's favorite books, such as a biography set of the previous presidents. At times, both Harrison and his first wife, Caroline, worked out of this room.

Cigar case
Despite his periodic attempts to quit, Harrison was fond of cigars. His friends gave him this velvet-lined cigar box when he was in the White House. The inlay on the lid leaves no doubt regarding its owner.

The cane starts with Washington at the top and ends with Harrison at the bottom.

Subject of caricature

Like most public figures, Harrison was frequently caricatured. This plaster statue of Harrison was made by one of his neighbors and presumed friends, Frank Allen Jr., likely in jest and not criticism.

Centennial cane

To mark the nation's 100th anniversary, Harrison was given this folk art ceremonial walking stick as he was the "Centennial President." It depicts the faces of previous presidents. Interestingly, names of some presidents are misspelled.

Harrison's workspace

This photo of the library from 1888 shows Harrison's favorite library table on the left. He even took it with him to the White House.

This walnut table has an inlaid leather top, and the edges are embossed in gold.

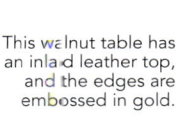

CARVING OF HARRISON

IN THE WHITE HOUSE

Although larger than the typical home, the White House felt crowded when Benjamin and Caroline Harrison arrived in 1889 because their children, grandchildren, and Caroline's father joined them in the second-floor family quarters. Only an unlocked door separated the family space from the crowded executive offices on the same floor—waiting room, telegraph room, Cabinet room, secretary's room, and the President's Office.

Adding to this, the Harrisons were always surrounded by a menagerie of pets, such as favorite dogs Dash and Jack. Grandson Baby McKee requested a goat, named Old Whiskers, which pulled the grandchildren in a goat cart. One day, while waiting beneath the portico for a carriage, Harrison was

Harrison Presidential China

Caroline designed her White House china with the American eagle in the center like President Lincoln's china. The cobalt rim is gilded with a braid of corn ears, stalks, and tassels—Caroline's distinctive touch.

surprised to discover Old Whiskers running down Pennsylvania Avenue—with Baby McKee in the attached cart. Everyone around was equally surprised to see their president, top hat in one hand and cane in the other, racing after and shouting at the goat. He reached and rescued his grandson just before the cart crashed into a ditch. The Harrisons owned some exotic animals, including alligators and two opossums named Mr. Reciprocity and Mr. Protection, but not all creatures were welcome in the White

House: on moving in, Caroline discovered rats and cockroaches, which were dealt with by an exterminator with ferrets. In a letter to her grandchildren, Caroline suggested that their new puppy could help catch the rats when he was big enough.

President Harrison took time in the afternoons to play with his grandchildren and pets on the White House lawn, and on occasion he slipped away to go on hunting or fishing trips. Devoted to the grandchildren, Harrison included them at dinners whenever possible, even when he was hosting visiting dignitaries.

Playtime for the Harrisons
Old Whiskers holds center stage on the White House lawn in this photograph. Russell Harrison holds the hand of his niece, Mary, while his nephew, Benjamin, and daughter, Marthena, ride in the cart. Dog Jack completes the family portrait.

Dolly Johnson
Laura "Dolly" Johnson, an African American cook from Kentucky, was employed to cater for the Harrisons, who did not like the rich food made by the previous cook. Dolly became nationally renowned for her cooking.

This reconstruction shows typical Victorian tree decorations, as well as actual presents to or from the family.

Family sitting room
This 1889 photograph shows the reception room, which the Harrisons usually used as the family sitting room. In the center of the room is the horn chair that was presented to the President by an admirer from Texas.

A White House Christmas
Christmas was important to the family. Caroline was the first First Lady to decorate a Christmas tree in the White House, in 1889, while Benjamin—a man that outsiders described as "aloof"—dressed up as Santa Claus for the grandchildren.

CIVIL WAR

"I am not a Julius Caesar, nor a Napoleon, but a plain Hoosier colonel," Harrison once wrote to his first wife, Caroline, in the midst of the Civil War that lasted from 1861 to 1865. Yet both his troops and his commanders considered him to be a dauntless soldier. Initially, however, he sat out the first year of conflict as he met the obligations of an elected official. Only after 1862, when President Lincoln called for more volunteers, did Harrison raise what became the 70th Indiana Regiment. He soon became its colonel.

For nearly two years, the regiment did little more than guard railroads, while its colonel drove himself hard and drilled his troops incessantly. From early 1864, the regiment got swept into the dramatic, hard-fought Atlanta Campaign that involved a series of battles. At the Battle of Resaca in northern Georgia, Harrison led the regiment in an assault on a rebel strongpoint and, after a ferocious hand-to-hand fight, won the day. At the Battle of Peachtree Creek, he commanded the brigade that halted a powerful Confederate attack and reversed the momentum of combat—this achievement would earn him the rank of brevet brigadier general. Toward the end of the campaign in 1864, Harrison proved to be instrumental in routing the rebel forces besieging Nashville, Tennessee.

After the Confederate surrender in April 1865, Harrison led his troops down Washington's Pennsylvania Avenue in the Grand Review of the Armies. After all, he had always been at the forefront.

Battle of Resaca, 1864
In one veteran's depiction of the pivotal Union attack at Resaca, Harrison's 70th Indiana can be seen at the top with the flag carrying the "70 IND" regiment number.

The canteen cup can be used to store the collapsed fork and spoon.

CANTEEN CUP

Prized possession
Harrison's officer's sword is festooned with shields and eagles. The Civil War service was a matter of pride for Harrison and, after the war, he kept his sword in the library.

Canteen set
These utensils, which were owned by Harrison, are probably made from a pewter alloy called Britannia metal. The Unionist manufacturers made a bewildering variety of simplified mess kits, most of which proved impractical on the field.

A hinge allowed the flatware to fold up.

FOLDED FORK

UNFOLDED SPOON

War veteran

This photographic portrait from 1865 depicts battle-hardened General Harrison. While affectionately nicknamed "Little Ben" by his troops, his friends and loyalists addressed him as the General for the rest of his life.

Brigadier General Commission

On January 23, 1865, President Abraham Lincoln signed this nomination of Harrison to be promoted to brevet brigadier general.

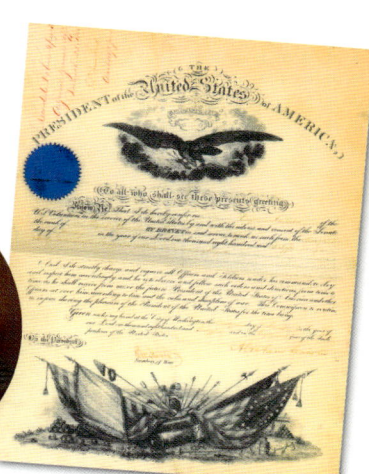

ABRAHAM LINCOLN

DINING ROOM

The dining room rivaled the front parlor as the most public space of the Harrisons' house throughout Benjamin Harrison's politically active years. During the weeks of the 1888 "Front Porch" campaign, when his doors were always open, hundreds if not thousands of people filed through the dining room, where the table was always replete with refreshments.

Even when the doors were closed to the public, fellow politicians, cabinet members, advisors, diplomats, journalists, and other influential men sat around this table to dine, discuss, and plan the future ahead. The 12 matching dining room chairs still seen today are in sturdy American Eastlake style. Made of walnut, these chairs are amply upholstered in the seats and backs.

Today, the room seems little changed despite the passage of more than a century. Plates are always set and decorative food is on the table. In a china cabinet against the wall some porcelain catches the eye: pieces from the Lincoln China—souvenirs from the Harrisons' days in the White House.

Love for oysters
During the Civil War, Harrison developed a taste for oysters after finding fresh river oysters near his camp. He retained his fondness of them for the rest of his life.

VICTORIAN OYSTER PLATE

This pitcher and goblet were a gift from the Glenwood (Iowa) Ladies Republican Club.

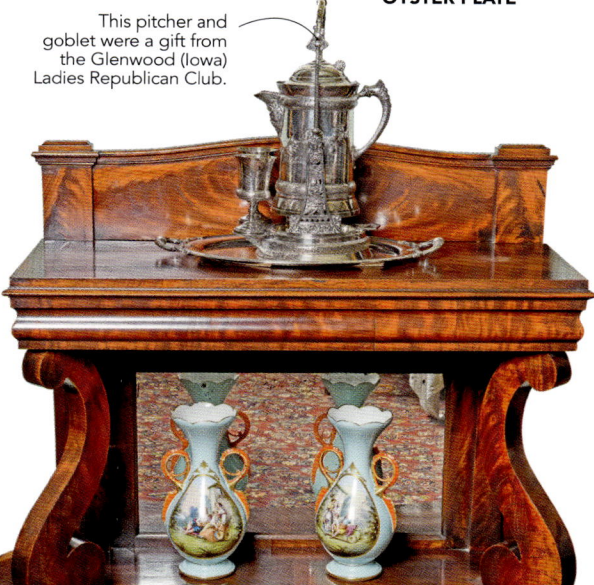

Serving table
The serving table and sideboard are made of mahogany. The ornate silver pitcher and goblet displayed on top were used in the White House.

The sideboard
This Empire-styled sideboard was bought by Caroline Harrison in Washington D.C., along with the matching serving table. Both feature mirrors to reflect candlelight and add a sense of depth to the room.

Women's heads form part of the handles, while the feet resemble bearded men

Coffee urn
This large urn is part of a silver tea and coffee set from 1887. Its typically Victorian style features engraved leaves and heads on the handles and feet.

Hosting parties

The dining room is large enough to easily accommodate the eight-leaf dining table and its 12 dining chairs. The table commands the room, in good company with the ornate fireplace, mirror, and chandelier.

WORKS OF ART

The Harrison home is replete with items collected by the family throughout the course of their lives. There are portraits of ancestors—including Harrison's grandfather, the nation's ninth president, William Henry Harrison—as well as works of art rendered by friends and acquaintances. These include Jacob Cox, a noted landscape and portrait artist, who painted a banner for Harrison's grandfather's 1840 presidential campaign, and T.C. Steele, a prominent member of the "Hoosier Group" of Impressionist painters from Indiana, who painted Harrison's portrait after his return from the White House.

The Harrison family also received gifts and curios from admirers and well-wishers. Harrison's wooden portrait, created in 1892 by someone known only as "M.V.M.," is but one example. Jonathan Eastman Johnson, a well-known painter from New York, also created a full-length portrait of Harrison in 1895, which is included in the White House collection of presidential portraits.

The artworks owned by the Harrisons are displayed at the Site today alongside others from the same time period, including many from the talented and prolific hand of Caroline Harrison.

The original watercolor sketch, made by Tiffany Studios designer Frederick Wilson, shows the full extent of the stained-glass window.

Angel of the Resurrection
This stained-glass window was commissioned by Harrison's second wife, Mary, in his memory in 1901. Made by Tiffany Studios for the First Presbyterian Church in Indianapolis, it can now be found at the Indianapolis Museum of Art at Newfields.

Bronze figurine
This Art Nouveau statue of a lady holding aloft an olive branch is likely a copy of the original, which was sculpted in France by Felix Charpentier in the late 19th century. While it is not known when the Harrisons acquired the piece, it has been on display in the front hallway for many years.

The Last of the Buffalo, 1891
This photogravure, or photograph etched on metal plate, of Albert Bierstadt's 1888 oil painting is an allegorical representation of the near extinction of the American bison. It was presented to Caroline by the artist himself.

nat sleepest:

Arise from   the dead : and

Christ shall   give thee light

Folk art

U.S. presidents were frequent subjects for folk artists. This 3-foot-tall hand-carved plaque was created by an "M.V.M." and features the visage of Harrison surrounded by 13 stars, representing the original 13 U.S. states.

Idyllic landscape

Jacob Cox (1810—1892) was a major figure among Indiana's 19th century artists. This painting by Cox is thought to portray Pogue's Run, now an urban creek, in Indianapolis.

KITCHEN

The kitchen and pantry of the Harrisons' home were part of the servants' area, seldom seen by guests. Overseen by Caroline, these were workspaces, the kitchen being largely devoted to the preparation of meals and the feeding of the children. It also served as the dining area for the servants. Other chores were undertaken here as well, such as laundry and churning cream into butter.

On the opposite wall from the butter churn and icebox was a freestanding cookstove, which ran on coal until it was converted to gas in the 1890s. Although the Harrisons eventually wired the house for electricity, the oak-paneled icebox still relied on the blocks of ice in the insulated upper chambers to cool food in the lower ones. The darker Hoosier cabinet, first marketed in Indiana in 1898, would become a very popular kitchen storage unit all over the United States throughout the early 20th century.

Birdcage
Harrison's house was home to many pets. The birdcage housed Caroline's feathered friends, which she frequently depicted in her paintings.

Rabbit spoon
This large serving or mixing spoon belonged to Caroline. The handle's nickel-silver tip features an image of a scampering rabbit.

Grocery list
A rare, handwritten relic from the past, this shopping list shows what the Harrisons ate: steak, lamb chops, beef tongue, cantaloupe, and other melons.

Victorian kitchen
The kitchen has elements of elevated Victorian design, such as the paneled sink with its pump-operated iron faucet. Even Baby McKee's high chair has an engraved tray.

PANTRY

A common feature in the upper-class houses of late 19th and early 20th centuries was the butler's pantry. It was used to store the valuable silver—traditionally under the butler's care—as well as other tableware such as linen, glasses, serving dishes, candles, and even wine. It was also the place where the staff would decide how the meals would be presented to the guests.

In the Harrison household, the pantry was the link between the busy kitchen where food was prepared and cooked and the elegant dining room, where the Harrisons and their guests conversed or debated as they were served their meals, candlelight reflecting from the polished silver, crystal goblets, and exquisite china. The pantry was expanded in 1895.

Space for storage
A butler's pantry was usually dominated by large cabinets in which the fine china cups and plates were stored, alongside the silver, glass, and other tableware.

Remnant of the past
An iron burn on the pantry sideboard was not sanded down during restoration but was instead left as a memento of one otherwise forgotten domestic accident.

Caroline's canvas
Caroline Harrison was swept up in the late-19th-century trend of painting on china or porcelain. Her expertise is apparent in these exquisite depictions of birds and flowers.

This gold-trimmed ribbon plate features intertwined purple and lavender pansies.

This painting of a Baltimore oriole shows Caroline's skill with the brush.

CAROLINE HARRISON'S ART

Caroline Harrison showed her artistic talent from a young age. Growing up in the small college town of Oxford, Ohio, she excelled in drawing as well as music and literature, owing to the encouragement of her family.

In Indianapolis, Caroline picked up the skill of china and porcelain painting. She exhibited pieces in several years of the Indiana Exposition, twice winning first prize. Her art improved under the tutelage of artist Paul Putzki, her instructor, who would later help her design the Harrison White House china collection. This caused minor controversy as she chose French Limoges china, while her President husband actively supported tariffs on the import of foreign goods in order to protect American industries.

Caroline turned her hand to painting in other mediums as well, such as oil painting. In 1886, Benjamin Harrison—a senator at the time—worried that her recent spell of serious illness was due to her "constantly working on … tapestry painting."

In the White House, Caroline pursued her interests with impressive vigor along with all her official duties as the First Lady, and even had an artist's studio set up in the attic. Flowers were her favorite subject, and she made studies of those that were new to her. Orchids were not found in Indiana at that time, but she personally cultivated some in the White House conservatory. She loved chrysanthemum flowers and also painted many other garden varieties including pansies, roses, nasturtiums, sweet peas, and four-leaf clovers. These adorned the many decorated porcelain gifts she gave away to friends, each dish signed "C.S. Harrison" or simply "CSH." Such was her passion for painting that she even painted magnolias on a porcelain bathtub for her grandson Benjamin.

Yellow Orchid

Caroline's favorite flowers to paint were orchids. This depiction of a yellow-flowering orchid was the last watercolor she produced before her death.

Tea with flowers

Caroline painted this three-piece tea set with morning glory and a serving tray with orchids around 1890. She painted with a broad brush, attributing much of the delicacy of the work to this technique.

This fairy hides his eyes just like children would have done at the traditional Easter egg hunt on the White House lawns.

Easter egg

With a careful hand, Caroline decorated fragile eggshells in addition to china and porcelain. This example still survives more than a century after it was made.

Lifelike butterflies painted in gold

Chocolate pot
This square chocolate pot was a gift from Caroline to her friend Ethel Johnson Hurty, hence the monogram features an intertwined "E" and "H."

Peaches
While Caroline preferred watercolors, this still-life oil-on-canvas painting of peaches spilling from a basket shows that she was adept at rendering depth and texture across different art mediums.

The handles on the set resemble plant stems.

The tray's orchids match the tea set's morning glory vines in style, color, and tone.

MARY'S ROOM

A framed photograph on the nightstand announces that this room belonged to Mary Scott Harrison, Benjamin Harrison's older daughter. Her bedstead was carved from walnut and adorned with beaded trim. Born in Indianapolis in 1858, Mary was known to be an affectionate girl, always close to her parents.

After Harrison was elected to the U.S. Senate in 1881, Mary went to Washington with him whenever the Congress was in session. Her marriage to James Robert McKee in 1884 did not alter this way of life. The newlyweds lived in the Delaware Street house, where the dressing room adjacent to this room could easily be turned into a nursery for her two children, Benjamin and Mary. Along with her brother and his family, they all moved into the White House on Harrison's election.

Mary acted as the secretary to her mother, Caroline. After Caroline died in October 1892, Mary, a born hostess, became the acting First Lady of the United States for the remainder of her grieving father's term. She accompanied him back to Indianapolis and helped him redecorate, upgrade, and electrify the house. The close parental bond was only ruptured in 1896 when Harrison chose to wed Mary's own first maternal cousin, Mary Lord "Mame" Dimmick.

A plumed gift
Made of ostrich feathers, the fan on the mantel was a gift to Caroline from Ida Grant, daughter-in-law of Gen. Ulysses S. Grant. Such accessories were so popular at this time that a "fan language" evolved consisting of perhaps two dozen subtle gestures.

Baptism certificate
Dated June 1, 1889, this document is the certificate of baptism for Mary's daughter and Harrison's granddaughter, Mary Lodge McKee.

The certificate has Harrison's entire cabinet as witnesses.

A grand bedroom

Mary's room reflects Victorian grandeur with its canopied bed and ornate fireplace. The wallpaper, although not original, is typical of the period. Adjacent to this room is a small room used as a dressing room or nursery.

The cape is trimmed with ostrich feathers.

Harrison's baby bed

The crib in this photograph taken at the White House is a Harrison heirloom. Made of walnut in the Sheraton style, it has cradled several generations of infants, including the president and his grandchildren.

Mary's cape

Mary wore this cape on the occasion of being presented to the Court of St. James in London while on a three-month tour of Europe in the summer of 1891. She traveled with her sister-in-law May Saunders Harrison.

ELIZABETH'S ROOM

Elizabeth Harrison was Harrison's third surviving child and only offspring from his second marriage. Elizabeth was born in 1897; tragically, Harrison died shortly after she turned four. She mostly spent her childhood in the Indianapolis house and attended school at Tudor Hall (now Park Tudor). When Elizabeth was 16, she moved to New York City with her mother, Mary Dimmick Harrison.

This room is interpreted as Elizabeth's childhood bedroom and includes images of her childhood days spent in the home. Decades would pass before the house would open to the public as a memorial to the 23rd president of United States. Fortunately, most of the furniture was still intact, with 75–80 percent of all furnishings in the home original to the Harrisons themselves.

Elizabeth graduated from New York University School of Law and made a success of life in New York. A popular financial journalist, she was the only woman to serve on the Committee for Economic Development, a renowned think tank. In 1921 she married James Blaine Walker, Jr., the grandson of Harrison's Secretary of State, James Blaine. They had two children, Benjamin and Jane. Elizabeth Harrison Walker died in 1955 at the age of 58.

Young Elizabeth
This photograph, taken in Paris, France, in 1899 shows two-year-old Elizabeth with her doting father. Benjamin Harrison was in Paris in his role as a lawyer, representing Venezuela in court over a boundary dispute with Great Britain.

Elizabeth's bedroom
The woman in the painting hanging on the wall is Elizabeth herself. It was painted in the 1920s by Virginia Keep Clark, a fellow resident from Old Northside, and added to the room at a later date.

Versatile room
Floral wallpaper, a coal-burning grate, and a beautifully inlaid and veneered drop-front desk lend an air of elegant repose to the sitting room.

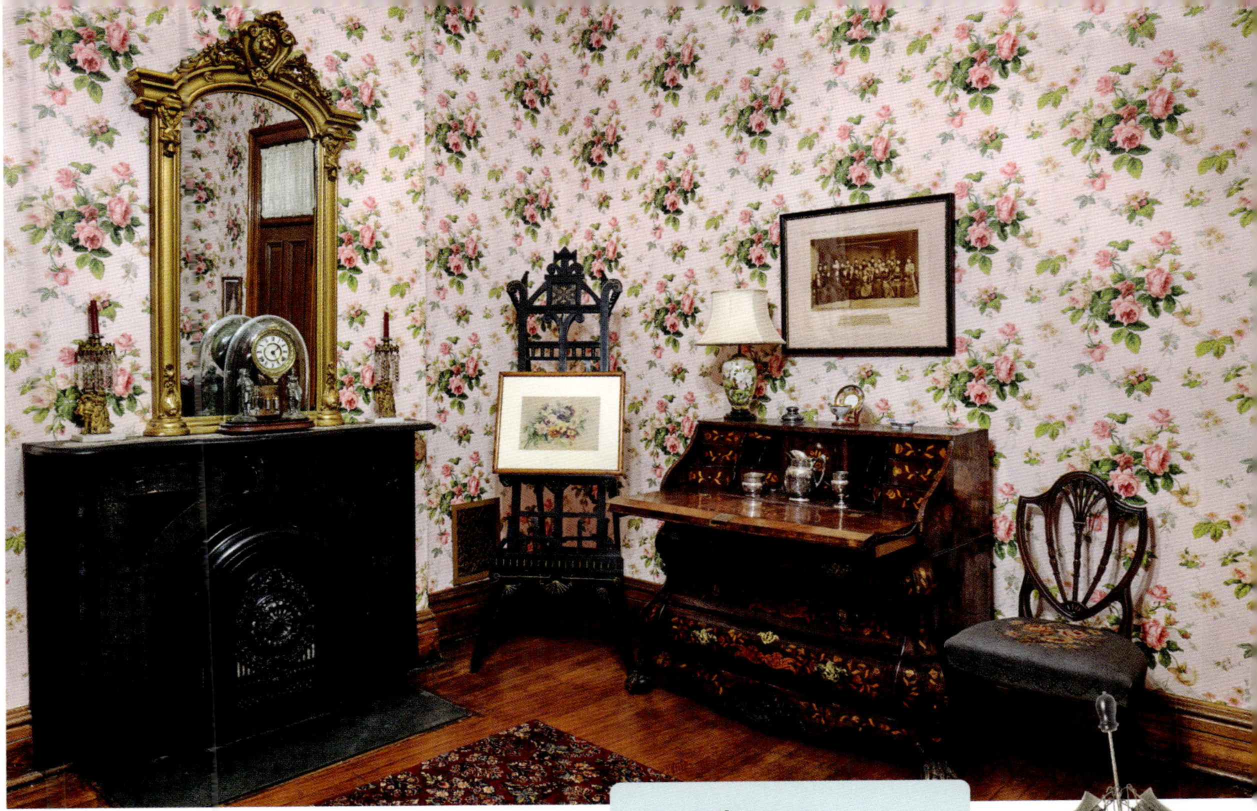

SITTING ROOM

The term "sitting room" refers to a small, comfortable, and intimate room that can serve many purposes. During Caroline Harrison's lifetime, this room served alternately as a boudoir and a workspace for her chambermaid and seamstress. It could also be used as a project room for making Christmas or birthday presents, addressing cards, knitting socks and mittens, or for needlepoint work. It also served as the getaway room for reading or simply for conversation between women. At one point, Mary Harrison McKee, Harrison's daughter from his first marriage, used it as an additional bedroom.

Such all-purpose rooms were often the repositories of excess furniture too fine or interesting for the attic but not demanded elsewhere. The sitting room still keeps its secrets as well as its charm.

1892

Dear Mrs. Harrison;
Please
receive these sweet
messengers of the south
and let them speak to
you in voices soft and
low of the love and
tender sympathy of a
little unknown friend.
Helen Keller
Tuscumbia, October fifteenth

For
Mrs. Harrison.
The White House
Washington,
D.C.

Helen Keller was born
in Tuscumbia, Alabama,
in 1880.

Personal correspondence
This letter was sent to Caroline by 12-year-old Helen Keller, who triumphed over her auditory-visual disability to become a famed author and activist.

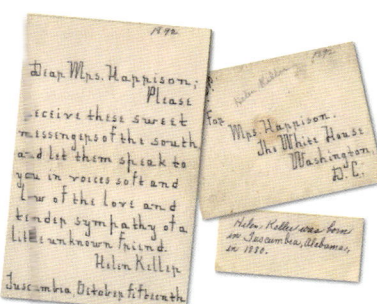

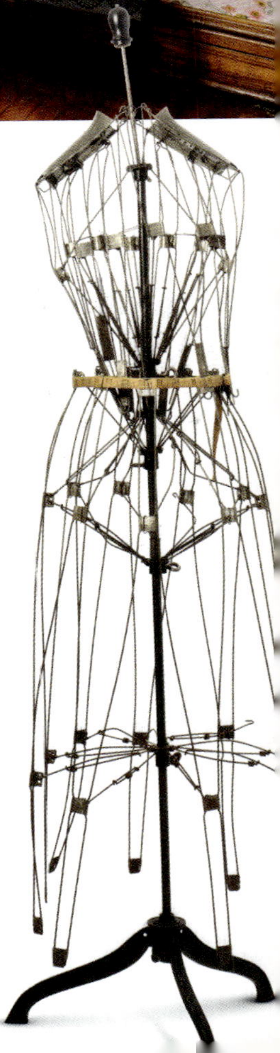

A model figure
Dress forms such as this were used by seamstresses to create or alter dresses for the Harrison ladies.

FIRST LADY OF FIRSTS

Caroline Lavinia Scott, known as Carrie, was born in 1832 in Oxford, Ohio. Clever and talented, she earned a degree in music, art, and literature from the Oxford Female Institute in 1852 and was a music instructor before marrying Benjamin Harrison in 1853. Even while supporting him and raising their children, Caroline was involved in her local church, taught Sunday school, and set up the Widows and Orphans Friends Society in Indianapolis after the Civil War.

Caroline assisted in the design and build of the 16-room house in Indianapolis, where her art would later grace the walls. After Harrison was elected president in 1888, Caroline went beyond her role of a White House hostess. With the extended Harrison family in the White House, the cramped family quarters were deemed intolerable. Caroline made

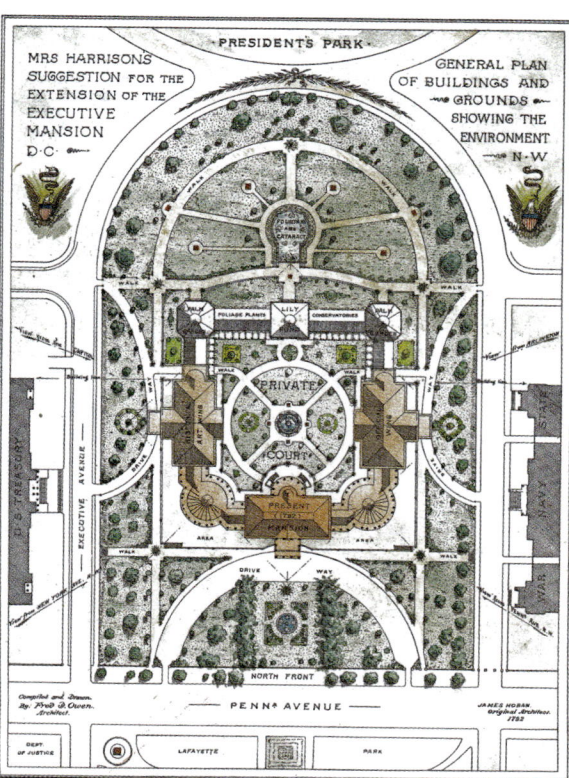

DAR Insignia pin

This Insignia pin, owned by Caroline's daughter Mary, features a compass with 13 points capped with gems to represent the 13 Founding States. They are arranged clockwise in order of when each colony ratified the U.S. Constitution.

renovations, the key improvement being the installation of electricity. She then poured herself into a grand redesign of the entire presidential complex, but the Congress refused to fund it. Undeterred, Caroline established the White House china collection after retrieving the china left behind by the previous administrations. She personally designed the Harrison china using the eagle on the Lincoln china for inspiration. She was concerned that historical objects had not been kept from previous administrations and made an inventory of such artifacts that were in the White House.

Meanwhile, the newly formed Daughters of the American Revolution (DAR), for women who were direct descendants of patriots of the Revolution, elected the First Lady as their first President General, owing to her commitment to historic preservation. Her name also stood her in good stead when she petitioned Johns Hopkins Medical School to allow women to enroll, and raised funds for them to do so.

Caroline Harrison was 60 years old when she died of tuberculosis in the White House on October 25, 1892, with her family at her bedside.

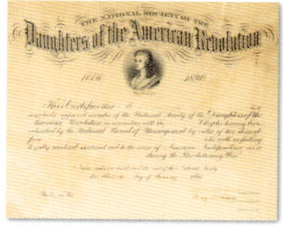

In good company

As the DAR's President General, Caroline signed this membership certificate. Another signature belongs to Eugenia Washington, great-grand niece of George Washington.

White House restoration plan

Caroline and architect Frederick D. Owen planned for a major expansion of the White House, complete with colonnades and even a greenhouse—a plan that the Congress refused to fund.

Larger than life
This portrait of Caroline by Daniel Huntington was commissioned by the DAR posthumously. It was presented to the White House in 1894, and a copy was given to the museum in the 1930s. Notice that Caroline is wearing her Insignia pin on her lapel.

THE HARRISONS' BEDROOM

The primary bedroom witnessed momentous family milestones. It is where Harrison's youngest child, Elizabeth, was born; it is also where the former president died.

The room is dominated by a bed with massive bedframe, its headboard alone standing eight feet tall. It was made from satinwood and rosewood in the Renaissance Revival style in around 1875. A matching marble-topped dresser with mirror and several chairs complete the set, brought to the house by his second wife, Mary Dimmick Harrison.

Harrison was confined to this bed during his last days. In early March 1901, Harrison came down with what seemed like a cold. A few days later, he was sitting at the breakfast table when a severe chill seized him, which turned out to be the first sign of pneumonia. He fought for days, his fever once spiking to more than 102°F (39°C), but there was little physicians or friends could do. His wife, Mary, was keeping a stoic vigil when, in the gloomy late afternoon of March 13, 1901, the former president died quietly in her arms. He was 67 years old. Harrison's body lay in state in the Indiana Statehouse before being buried next to his first wife, Caroline, in Crown Hill Cemetery in Indianapolis.

PIN TRAY

JEWELRY BOX

HAIRBRUSH

MIRROR

BUTTONHOOK

Repoussé dresser set
Caroline owned and used this matching set of exquisitely adorned grooming tools made with the silversmithing technique of chasing and repoussé. Owning a set from precious silver was a sign of status.

HARRISON'S 1888 CAMPAIGN RIBBON

Personal patch
Crazy quilts were popular in the 1800s. The quilt on the Harrisons' bed includes ribbons from his successful election campaign in 1888.

The Harrison children

This portrait of Benjamin and Caroline's children, Russell (1854–1936) and Mary (1858–1930), hangs in the master bedroom. Their third child, a daughter, died at birth.

Classical design

The imposing bedframe, inspired by ancient Egyptian and Roman features, has a large cartouche of Egyptian queen Cleopatra. The chairs are also topped by Cleopatra or her lover, Mark Antony.

Family holiday

This photo of Benjamin, Mary, and Elizabeth sits in the bedroom. It was taken at Francklyn Cottage in Elberon, New Jersey—a popular vacation choice of many late-19th-century presidents.

Home gymnasium

Despite a busy schedule, Harrison still managed to find time for exercise with his "Whitney Home Gymnasium," which traveled with him to the White House. Patented in 1882, the portable gymnasium includes dumbbells, resistance clubs, and pulleys.

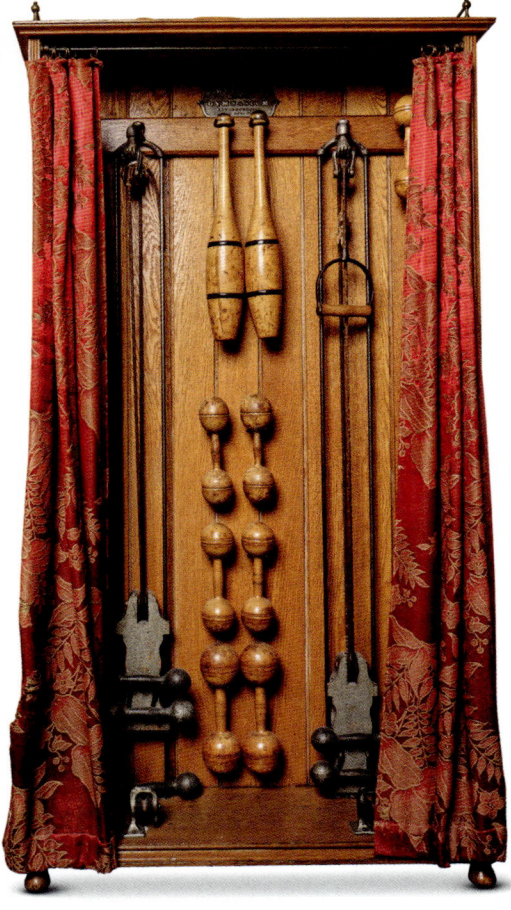

THE LAWYER

Like many new lawyers beginning their careers, a young Benjamin Harrison struggled to establish a viable legal practice. However, in 1855, he formed a partnership with William Wallace that brought them numerous clients and a steady paycheck. After his service in the Civil War, Harrison was able to resume his practice successfully on his return to Indianapolis.

Throughout his career, Harrison argued 15 cases before the U.S. Supreme Court, including six when serving in the Senate. The cases usually pivoted on constitutional questions regarding the seizure of private property, municipal boundary considerations, and inheritance tax laws. Such complex cases led to increased renown locally and nationally.

After his presidency, Harrison still had a legal career to pursue. In 1899, he served as senior counsel to Venezuela in a dispute with Great Britain over borders with British Guiana, arguing before the

Changing tides

Over the years Harrison's partnership changed its composition, and in 1874 it became Harrison, Miller & Elam, its most enduring name. Their offices were located at Wright's Block in Indianapolis.

Harrison's law office

This recreation of Harrison's law office is located on the third floor of the Benjamin Harrison Presidential Site. The setting features his original furniture, including many drawers and shelves for documents, and a desk on castors that could fold closed.

International Court of Arbitration in Paris. While Harrison lost the prominent case, it further bolstered his reputation as a lawyer. Remarkably, the border dispute remains contested to this day.

Harrison was named as one of the top lawyer presidents by the American Bar Association, which included other notables such as John Adams, Grover Cleveland, and Martin Van Buren. The author Harry Lambeth said Harrison had a "brilliant mind, extraordinary memory, unusual powers of analysis, and great speaking ability."

The lawyer's office
Between 1875 and 1898, Harrison's law firm was located in the Wright's Block building in downtown Indianapolis. This photograph of the building, taken during Harrison's 1888 presidential campaign, shows windows and balustrades draped in bunting. Such was the support Harrison had garnered.

The Cold Spring Murders
In 1868, Nancy Clem (among others) was charged with the double murder of Jacob and Nancy Young at Cold Spring in Marion County, Indiana. The jury at Clem's first trial was hung, but Harrison led the prosecution at the second trial. He called more than 250 witnesses, and proved that Clem's alibi came from a bribed witness. His final argument lasted eight hours. The jury found Clem guilty—the first woman to be convicted of murder in Indiana.

Lengthy proceedings
In 1895, Harrison represented the plaintiffs in the Morrison Will Case that was tried in Richmond, Indiana. Spanning over five months, this case was one of the longest jury trials on record.

FROM THE VAULT

The Benjamin Harrison Presidential Site holds more than 11,000 artifacts in its vaults. While it is practically impossible to display all of them, some favorites are featured here. Two noteworthy motifs stand out. The first is the log cabin, long the symbol of the early American frontier. Contrary to popular assumption, Benjamin and his grandfather William Henry Harrison were not born in simple log cabins; rather, they were referred to as "log cabin candidates." Democrats cast William Henry Harrison as an out-of-touch, provincial old man who would rather "sit in his log cabin drinking hard cider" than attend to the administration of the country. This strategy backfired when Harrison adopted the log cabin as his campaign symbol. The other motif is the top hat, associated with Harrison's grandfather and used in the 1888 election campaign alongside the slogan, "Grandfather's hat fits Ben too." His political enemies turned the theme on its head—Democratic cartoonists drew tiny Benjamins in huge top hats, visually declaring he could never live up to his grandfather's standards.

Baby McKee's high chair
This Victorian chair that stands in the kitchen today is known to have been used by Harrison's daughter Mary when feeding her infant son, Benjamin "Baby" Harrison McKee. The center of the tray is inscribed with his name and date of birth, October 22, 1887.

Centennial cylinder
This ornate silver Tiffany & Co. case was presented to Harrison, the "Centennial President," as part of the celebrations of 100 years since George Washington's presidency. As inscribed on the front of the cylinder, it contains the "Address to the President of the United States, by the representatives of the Civil, Industrial & Commercial Bodies of N.Y. City."

THE ADDRESS ON A SCROLL INSIDE

Dog whistle
Avid animal lovers, the Harrison family had at least one pet dog at any given time. This pewter whistle with a dog's face features eyes made of gemstone. It belonged to Harrison's grandson, Baby McKee, whose initials are engraved on it.

Grandfather's hat

This novelty of a baby in an oversized top hat originated as an insult, suggesting that Harrison could not fill his presidential grandfather's top hat, much less be effective as president. The song, however, was a pro-Harrison piece, even though the composer remained anonymous.

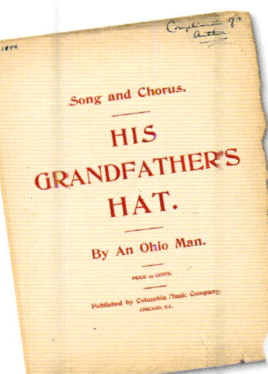

"HIS GRANDFATHER'S HAT" SHEET MUSIC

The pewter tray is engraved with birds, leaves, and flowers.

Grandfather's cabin

Log cabins always reminded Harrison of his grandfather's campaign. This metal cabin represents the one used to promote William Henry Harrison's presidential bid.

Plaque denotes the recipient as Reverend M.L. Haines, pastor of Indianapolis's First Presbyterian Church between 1885 and 1901.

LOG CABIN MOTIF

The wick would be fed by fuel within the hat's "stovepipe."

Haines' walking stick

This intricately carved walking stick was a Christmas gift in 1898 from Harrison to a close friend—the pastor of his Presbyterian church. Once again, a log cabin appears in prominent relief. Early Presbyterian churches on the frontier were made from logs of wood.

Top hat torch

This torch in the shape of a top hat would have sat atop a post while being carried in torchlight parades during Harrison's 1892 reelection bid. The top hat continued to be used by both sides even throughout the second election campaign.

Capitol memento

All kinds of objects were used as election "posters." This one, created for the 1888 campaign, is made from stones that come from the U.S. Capitol Building and the Washington Monument, making a connection between Harrison and the seat of government in the minds of voters.

Patriotically, the faces of Harrison and his running mate Morton are painted along with a 38-star flag.

FAMILY ALBUM

As much as Benjamin Harrison was nicknamed "the human iceberg" by his political colleagues, he was at heart a family man, living with his daughter Mary and her family, his son Russell's family, and his 90-year-old father-in-law, Dr. John Scott, in the White House. In 1891 *The Minneapolis Tribune* described his grandson, Baby McKee, as "the little man who tells the president what to do." The family bonds are clearly displayed in photographs from their personal archives, taken around the time that home photography was becoming popular among the masses.

At home in the White House

By 1889, Benjamin Harrison's daughter and daughter-in-law had three children between them living in the White House. Mary "May" S. Harrison's second child, William, was born in 1896.

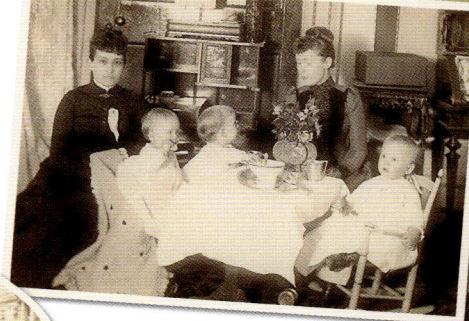

L–R: Mary Harrison McKee, Marthena "Martha" Harrison, Mary Lodge McKee, Mary "May" S. Harrison, Benjamin "Baby" McKee

The McKee family: mother Mary, daughter Mary, son Benjamin

DASH THE DOG

The family pets

Whether in Indiana or the White House, the Harrisons were never without pets. They had several dogs, including Jack, Spot, and Dash, the black and tan Collie, as well as opossums, alligators, birds, a lamb, and a goat.

MARY WITH A ST. BERNARD PUPPY

Three generations

Doting grandfather Harrison hugs Baby McKee as the child's mother, Mary, stands near. Unusually for an official portrait of this era, Harrison is smiling, revealing a kindness in his demeanor.

In the Adirondacks

In 1895, Harrison purchased a neck of land between two Adirondack lakes and built a summer home called Berkeley Lodge. It was a double-turreted log house with additional cabins and docks. From 1896, Harrison and his second wife, Mary Lord Dimmick Harrison, spent every summer there, often with friends.

THE LOOKOUT TOWER, CALLED *KIJKOVERAL* ("SEE OVER ALL")

IN FRONT OF BERKELEY LODGE

LAUNCHING THEIR BOAT, *THE ELIZABETH*

THE BOAT HOUSE

John P. Jackson was Harrison's friend since they were apprentices working for a Cincinnati law firm.

On vacation

In March 1894, the widower Harrison (seated at top) and his family were invited to spend Easter at Jackson's Napa Soda Springs, California, an extravagant resort established by his friend, Colonel John P. Jackson (standing in middle).

PRESIDENTIAL CONNECTIONS

As a public figure, Benjamin Harrison enjoyed an unusually rich web of connections with other famous Americans of the late 19th century. Of course, any president would have to be politically well connected; Harrison can be linked to 14 fellow presidents, ranging from his own grandfather to Herbert Hoover. Other acquaintances of note include Frederick Douglass, the African American abolitionist and social reformer; John Wanamaker, the Philadelphia department-store tycoon; and the Studebaker brothers, founders of the Studebaker automobile company, who supported Harrison in his 1888 presidential campaign. Clement Studebaker went on to serve on Harrison's Pan-American Conference committee.

Harrison also knew many prominent writers. Lew Wallace, a native of Indiana and author of *Ben-Hur*, wrote his campaign biography, *The Life of Gen. Ben Harrison*, in 1888. His brother, William Wallace, had a law partnership with Harrison from 1854 to 1860.

The poet James Whitcomb Riley was Harrison's friend and a part of his presidential campaign. Riley attended many White House functions; his recital in 1892 at the special request of Harrison was an occasion described as a "charming and handsome affair."

The Book of Joyous Children
James Whitcomb Riley, known as the "Hoosier Poet" and the "Children's Poet," published this collection of verse in 1902. It is known for its celebration of childhood innocence.

Herbert Hoover
In 1894, a 19-year-old student and baseball fan met Harrison at Stanford University at a ball game hosted by the Stanford baseball team. The student was Herbert Hoover, who later became the 31st president of the United States.

Frederick Douglass
Formerly an enslaved man, Douglass went on to become a well-known civil rights advocate, activist, writer, and public speaker. President Harrison appointed him as the ambassador to the Republic of Haiti.

President's carriage
Harrison never owned an automobile, but he did use carriages. Aiming to support Indiana businesses, he ordered five Brougham carriages from the Studebaker Brothers for use at the White House.

DECLARATION OF INDEPENDENCE
JOHN TRUMBULL

Historic moment
On July 4, 1776, delegates representing the 13 original colonies adopted the Declaration of Independence. Harrison was related to five of the seven signers from Virginia. In this painting, Benjamin Harrison V—great-grandfather of President Benjamin Harrison—is seated at the table on the far left.

This full-size copperplate engraving is a reproduction of the original Declaration and was made by William J. Stone in 1823.

Harrison's fourth great-grandfather, Benjamin Harrison II, is the great-grandfather of three signers, Benjamin Harrison V, Richard Henry Lee, and Francis Lightfoot Lee. Carter Braxton and Thomas Nelson descended from Robert Carter, another of Harrison's ancestors. The signatures of the five kindred signers are clustered around that of Thomas Jefferson, the Declaration's principal author.

IN CONGRESS. JULY 4, 1776.

The unanimous Declaration of the thirteen united States of America.

LEGACY

Every American president leaves behind a record of accomplishments that have shaped the nation. Benjamin Harrison, for example, markedly expanded the scope of foreign policy, especially regarding Latin America, with the creation of the Pan-American Conference. He modernized the U.S. Navy—which had just two armored cruisers in 1888—by initiating a shipbuilding campaign that provided the Navy with 19 new vessels mounting 12-inch and 10-inch guns, with 18 more under construction. Remembering the

Civil War, Harrison encouraged national unity through flying the U.S. flag and reciting the Pledge of Allegiance. He also fought strongly for protecting Black civil rights. Perhaps most forward-thinking of all, his presidency was conservation-oriented. He created the National Forest Reserve system, setting aside 13 million acres of the public domain to establish three National Parks: Yosemite, Sequoia, and General Grant (King's Canyon National Park).

Harrison and conservation
President Harrison implemented one of the most important pieces of U.S. conservation, the 1891 Forest Reserve Act—the foundation of 154 National Forests today, covering more than 294,000 square miles.

Harrison statue
Rapid City, South Dakota—a state established by Harrison—is home to a life-sized bronze statue of Harrison feeding birds, an apt theme for a conservationist.

Lower Falls, Yellowstone National Park
Harrison visited Yellowstone three times and, through the Forest Reserve Act, created a protective buffer around the park—the Yellowstone Park Timberland Reserve, today's Yellowstone National Forest.

Grand Canyon, Arizona
Although Harrison never visited the Grand Canyon, he hoped to establish a national park there. He had to settle for creating a forest reserve instead in 1893. In 1919, the Grand Canyon became a national park.

States joining the Union

During President Harrison's term (1889–1893), six territories became full-fledged U.S. states. North Dakota, South Dakota, Montana, and Washington were admitted into the Union in November 1889. Eight months later, Idaho and Wyoming also gained statehood. No other single presidential term could claim more admissions. As a result, twelve new Republican Senators were soon embarking for Washington, which was a political bonus for Harrison's party.

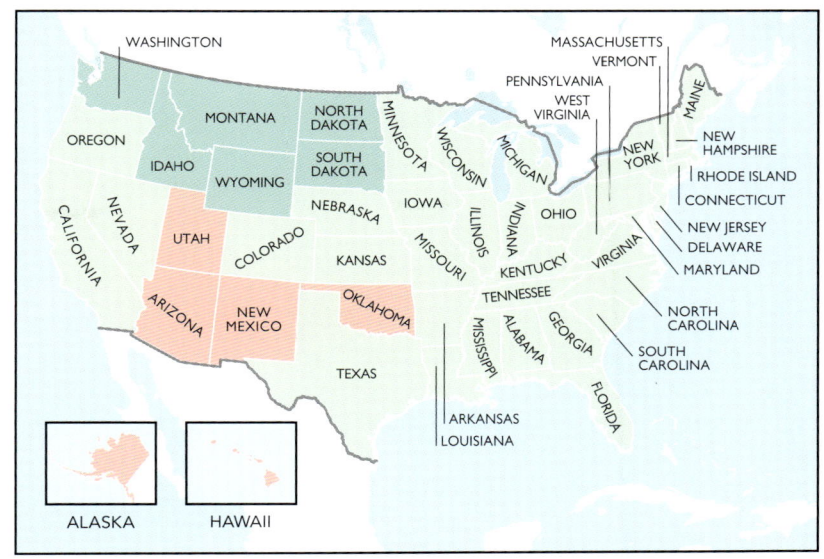

KEY

- Part of the union
- States formed under Harrison
- Not yet a part of the union

African American rights

In 1892, Frederick Douglass (fourth from right) accompanied President Harrison (sixth from left) for the unveiling of the Soldiers and Sailors Monument in Rochester, New York. Harrison supported legislation securing African American civil rights, but Congress failed to pass any measures.

HENRY WOOD ELLIOTT'S *THE SEAL ISLANDS OF ALASKA*

This book, from 1882, was used by Harrison during the preparation of Proclamation 287.

Northern Fur Seal, Alaska

Harrison was the first U.S President to protect an endangered animal species. He signed Proclamation 287, which barred the hunting of fur-bearing animals in Alaska and the Bering Strait.

NOTABLE QUOTATIONS

Harrison was an accomplished orator and writer from an early age. His essay "Composition No.9"—full title "Some of the Leading Differences in the Modes of Living, Labor and Enjoyment of the Comforts of Life in a Savage and a Highly Advanced State of Society"—was written when he was just 16 years old. His politics of fairness for all continued right through to his Annual Messages to Congress (today called the State of the Union address).

*"**Great lives** do not go out, they **go on**."*

SPEECH IN NEW YORK STATE, AUGUST 1891

*"Let those who would **die for the flag** on the field of battle give a better proof of their **patriotism** and a higher glory to their country by promoting **fraternity** and **justice**."*

INAUGURAL ADDRESS, MARCH 1889

Official portrait
This is the official White House portrait of President Benjamin Harrison. It was painted by Jonathan Eastman Johnson in 1895, two years after Harrison's term in office. It is notable that his chosen pose includes books.

This unofficial 42-star flag was made after the state of Washington's admission to the Union in 1889.

*"The manner by which **women are treated** is a good criterion to judge the **true state** of society."*

COLLEGE ESSAY "COMPOSITION NO.9," 1849

*"I have **traversed this broad land** of ours, and out of all this journeying, out of all this **mingling with our people**, I have come to be a prouder and, I hope, **better American**."*

SPEECH IN COLORADO SPRINGS, MAY 1891

*"**No worthy end** or cause can be promoted by **lawlessness**."*

FOURTH ANNUAL MESSAGE, DECEMBER 1892

*"No other people have a government more worthy of their respect and love or a **land so magnificent** in extent, so pleasant to look upon, and so full of generous suggestion to **enterprise and labor**."*

INAUGURAL ADDRESS, MARCH 1889

*"I pity the man who wants a coat so cheap that the man or woman who produces the cloth will **starve in the process**."*

SPEECH IN VERMONT, AUGUST 1891

*"The emancipation proclamation was heard in the depths of the earth as well as in the sky; **men were made free**, and material things became our **better servants**."*

INAUGURAL ADDRESS, MARCH 1889

*"When and under what conditions is the Black man to have a free ballot? When is he in fact to have those **full civil rights** which have so long been his in law?"*

FIRST ANNUAL MESSAGE, DECEMBER 1889

BENJAMIN HARRISON PRESIDENTIAL SITE

The Benjamin Harrison Presidential Site's mission is to increase public participation in the American system of self-government by sharing the life stories, arts, and culture of an American President. The Presidential Site's purpose is to preserve the nationally significant Harrison home and share the extensive collection as an educational museum and historical resource to promote public service, civil civic discourse, and good citizenship.

After the Harrisons' time, the building was bought by the Arthur Jordan Foundation, who committed to preserve it as a memorial to the 23rd president in perpetuity. That legacy lives on today through its

PRESIDENT Benjamin HARRISON MEMORIAL Home

Sign of the times
In 1966, the Harrison house became the President Benjamin Harrison Memorial Home. In 2010, it adopted its present name, the Benjamin Harrison Presidential Site.

partnership with the Benjamin Harrison Presidential Site and its focus on civic and history education. Tens of thousands of people visit annually, engaging in tours and programs linking the Harrison family to the greater American story and to events such as the signing of the Declaration of Independence, the opening of the Ellis Island Immigrant Station, and the adoption of the Pledge of Allegiance.

Schoolchildren are especially welcome at the Presidential Site, which offers field trips and resources for teachers. Students are encouraged to join youth leadership programs, such as the Future Presidents of America camp, with the aim of ensuring a new generation of civically engaged citizens.

A warm welcome
The N. Delaware Street entrance to the Presidential Site flies the flags of the nation and the state of Indiana. Visitors check in at the red-painted Welcome Center, a reconstruction of the carriage house behind the home.

RESEARCH LIBRARY

For scholars pursuing extensive studies in Benjamin Harrison's career or in Gilded Age America, the Presidential Site offers the services of the Harrison Family Presidential Research Library, which houses more than 10,000 historical items. Partially drawn from Benjamin Harrison's own personal library of newspapers, magazines, and artifacts, it also contains documents and objects acquired from other sources. These include political and presidential memorabilia, letters, historic photographs, household goods, clothing, and original artwork, among others. The collection spans decades and links the Harrison family to dozens of politicians, public figures, and more than 20 additional U.S. Presidents.

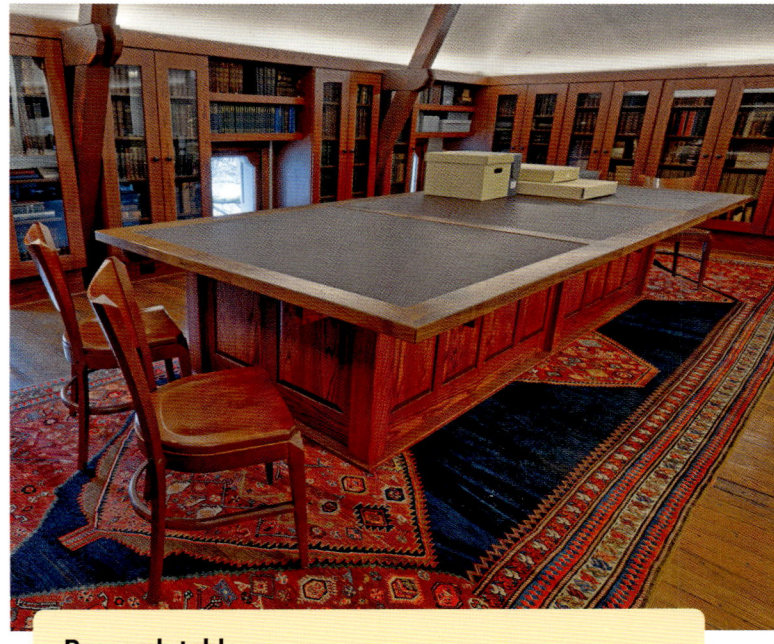

Research table
Inspired by Harrison's library table, this larger version in the Harrison Family Presidential Research Library is made of walnut and has an inlaid leather top, originally an easier surface for writing in longhand but today a decorative feature.

The letter is dated May 27, 1777, and was penned in Morristown, New Jersey, during the Revolutionary War.

WASHINGTON'S LETTER

George Washington letter
The Library holds unique items such as this letter from General George Washington to his new brigadier, General Anthony Wayne, hoping he could help stem desertion.

Library books
The Library's shelves are crowded with books, most of them from Harrison's own collections. They range from Civil War regimental histories, to legal tomes, compendia of statistics, atlases, and encyclopedic works.

Recipe book
Some items offer a unique window into 19th-century life. Caroline's well-used, handwritten recipe book features such delicacies as sugar cake, oyster pie, and "chocolate mange."

PRESIDENTIAL COMMONS

The Benjamin Harrison Presidential Site offers more than a tour of the former president's house. Its two-and-a-half-acre grounds also include a greenspace, memorial gardens, and a public commons honoring citizenship and statesmanship.

The area is far larger than the original gardens in Harrison's time. Benjamin Harrison purchased two lots of land in 1868; today, the plot extends north to E. 13th Street and south to the Bob Annis Way (E. 12th Street) on land where houses had previously stood on each side of the Harrisons' home. The area was extensively renovated in the early 2020s to develop the museum grounds.

Today, the south lawn is known as the Johnson-Floyd Family Presidential Commons. This area includes the Sarah Evans Barker Citizenship Plaza, which hosts a naturalization ceremony for new citizens every July. There is also the 89-ft tall Centennial Flagpole, echoing Harrison's call for the national flag to fly over every public building and school. His Presidential Proclamation 335 of 1892 says, "Let the national flag float over every schoolhouse in the country and the exercises be such as shall impress upon our youth the patriotic duties of American citizenship."

Walkway to the house
The granite and brick path leading from the Johnson-Floyd Family Presidentia Commons to the former president's house is known as the Stan and Sandy Hurt Presidential Promenade.

The welcome page says that the ceremony is "a fitting tribute" to Harrison, who "designated Ellis Island as the first federal immigration center" in 1890.

Capturing history
More than 1,600 people have taken the oath of citizenship at the Presidential Site. Since 2022, new citizens have the opportunity to have their name recorded in the stainless steel Book of History.

Footsteps of the founders
The promenade, lined with medallions that represent every president, allows visitors to follow the "footsteps of the founders."

Charters of Freedom

Visitors to the site are reminded of such principles as unalienable rights, rule of law, and limited government when they see these bronze reproductions of the founding documents of the United States: the Declaration of Independence, the U.S. Constitution, and the Bill of Rights.

All welcome

This portico marks entry into the Sarah Evans Barker Citizenship plaza, which is named for the federal judge who first performed the naturalization services at the Presidential Site.